Turn South at the Next Magnolia

DIRECTIONS FROM A
LIFELONG SOUTHERNER

Nan Graham

Coastal Carolina Press
Wilmington, North Carolina

Published by
Coastal Carolina Press
www.coastalcarolinapress.org

First Edition
Second Printing

Cover image: *The Road to Orton Plantation,* Kathleen Nobles
Magnolia art © 2000 www.arttoday.com
Design & composition by B. Williams and Associates

Library of Congress Cataloging-in-Publication Data
Graham, Nan, 1936–
Turn south at the next magnolia :
directions from a lifelong southerner / Nan Graham.—1st ed.
p. cm.
ISBN 1-928556-23-X
1. Southern States—Social life and customs—1865—Humor.
I. Title.
F216.2 .G7 2000
975'.04–dc21
00-047451

The essays in this book originally aired as commentaries on
Wilmington, N.C.'s local NPR affiliate, WHQR 91.3 FM.

Dedication

Dedicated with grateful affection and much love—To my children, Howell and Molly, their spouses, Debbie and Russ, grandbaby extraordinaire, Caroline, and especially to my long-suffering husband—Ernie, who swears he is *always* the "goat" of these commentaries. My family and friends have given inspiration and enormous joy to my life and—I hope—to my stories.

Acknowledgments

I am ever grateful to my editor, Emily Colin, and all at Coastal Carolina Press, who have been so kind and helpful; to Molly Graham Allred, Marie Tyndall, Knox Pierson, Maggie Aardema, Jane Grant, Sarah Jordan, Norma Norwood, and Carolyn Simmons, who listened with such good ears; to Roger Simmons, Tammy Mansur, Tamara Galloway, ace computer gurus who helped me tame the beast (or at least keep it at bay); to Martha Young Campbell who filled in the missing pieces; to Suzanne Ruffin, who always knows *le mot juste*, to my Writers' Group for their encouragement; and most especially to Aileen LeBlanc, (my first WHQR producer) and George Scheibner (my current WHQR producer), and *all* my WHQR family who have literally given me my "voice."

Contents

Introduction xi

PART I • GROWING UP SOUTHERN

Darning Needles and Croaker Sacks 3

South in the Mouth 6

Stamping White Horses and Keeping Cats 9

Advice from Mama 12

All God's Chillun 15

The Transplant 17

Ladies . . . Gentlemen . . . and Children of All Ages 19

The Centennial Time Traveler 21

Eclectic Eccentrics 23

Child of WWII 26

Southern Sisters 28

My Ten Cents' Worth 31

Riding the Dog 34

Food for Thought 37

Bread-and-Butter Notes 40

Lost and Found 42

Theaters of the Absurd 45

Hair Piece 47

Azalea Festival 1958 49

Off to Seek My Fortune 52

A Christmas Memoir in Three Parts:
Part I: Before Martha Stewart 54

PART II • GROWN UP SOUTHERN

Southern Choreography 61

Kith and Kin 63

The Subject of Snow 65

Cryptic Messages 67

Aelurophile 70

Boo! 73

Scratch and Sniff 76

Going Postal 79

Necessity: The Grandmother of Invention? 82

The Last Roundup 84

Baaa None 87

Floored 89

The Road to Livingston 91

Fits Like a . . . 93

Ring-a-Ling? 95

Taking Care of Business 98

Traffic Court 101

The Amazons 104

Hats Off 106

Adding Insult to Injury 108

The Purple Thumb 111

Dies Caniculares aka Dog Days 113

Foreign Languages 116

For Better or Worse 118

A Christmas Memoir in Three Parts:
Part II: Turkey Trauma 120

PART III • GROWING OLD SOUTHERN

Your Comments Please . . .   125

Girding the Loins or Gilding the Lions   128

A Dog for All Seasons   131

Iron Magnolia   134

Compu-Speak or "I Don't Do Windows"   137

Beach Cottage   140

Eh? What's That?   142

The Loop   144

The Fur Person   146

Fran and Other Lessons Learned   148

Hurricane Hangover   150

Floyd and the Chainsaw Chicken   152

Grandmère   154

Caroline Time   156

The Heart of the Matter   159

Like a Virgin   162

Luddite in Training   164

Bridge over Troubled Waters or The View from the Bridge   166

There's a Word for It   169

Journal Entry: Seagulls at Spring Break   171

Rodin Has Left the Building   173

The Christmas Spirits   175

A Christmas Memoir in Three Parts:
Part III: The Millennium Christmas   177

Introduction

The first WHQR commentary was "in the can." All that was left for this initial venture into Radioland was a "Lead In" and "Lead Out" for the announcer.

"And what do you want to use as your sign-off?" Aileen, the producer of the commentary segments, asked. "Usually the commentators give some credentials in the "Lead Out." She waited for me to answer.

I thought for a minute. "Well, I teach, of course." Somehow that didn't sound like a credential to recommend me for a radio job or as a commentator on the radio. "And my family . . . " my voice trailed off.

Aileen waited as if I were saving the best for last. Unfortunately, I wasn't. My mind was a blank. I thought about the commentary I had just taped, a piece called "Darning Needles and Croaker Sacks" on the changing South in a small Alabama town.

"And I'm a lifelong Southerner?" I suggested.

Aileen seemed pleased. "That's it," she said. And so it began. In January 1995, my biweekly four-minute commentaries started on public radio station WHQR. And I'm still at it today.

These years have given my writing a real electric cattle prod as well as the opportunity to explore characters and places in my past and in my present. My hook? The perspective of a Southern woman of a certain age who has lived through WWII, segregation, a race riot, cancer, thirty-nine years of marriage, the computer avalanche, a grandchild, the homogenization of our Southern setting into mainstream America, and more change than I thought possible. And it is my hope that the commentaries reflect a fresh view of the changes with a bit of humor to see it through.

PART ONE

Growing Up Southern

Darning Needles and Croaker Sacks

Southerners, like cats, are born with an exaggerated sense of place. We somehow feel connected to the small Southern towns, their customs and language, even though the recent decades have eroded the clear edges of what being Southern is all about. The small towns of Carolina, Georgia, Alabama and Mississippi, all had a certain familiar look until recently. The county seats were built around a red brick courthouse with an obelisk to the Confederate dead within a stone's throw of the front door.

My family was always moving when I was growing up, but fourteen of my summers were spent in Livingston, Alabama, where my grandmother lived. It was the county seat of Sumter County, where swings, seesaws, sliding boards, and a Boredwell were also in the square beside the Livingston Courthouse.

The Boredwell was an open arched pavilion with a fountain in the center for drinking and a spigot underneath the fountain to accommodate jugs and bottles. The evil-tasting mineral water from the spring below was touted as a tonic for everything from summer malaise to weak chins. Having a drink from the Boredwell was a prerequisite before you left the square after completing errands. It was part of Sumter County's health regimen.

Three or four tables in the Boredwell with wooden muleback chairs created a year-round oasis for domino players or anyone wanting to sit and cool himself.

The stores around the square satisfied all of the citizens' needs. McMillan's Bank, Mellan's General Store, the Rialto Theatre, and, of course, the Jitney Jungle, forerunner of today's supermarket. Almost all the stores had wide unvarnished floorboards which creaked satisfactorily when walked on.

Yes, the town looked a bit down at the heels, but it also had the well-worn patina of a weathered antique. The streets were always dusty but shaded by large hackberry and oak trees in the summertime. Traffic eased sluggishly along the streets, pedestrians zigzagging to their necessary stops without looking either way.

A favorite spot and social center on the square was Scruggs for Drugs, where Joe Scruggs presided over the sleek marble fountain top. Joe always looked fresh and starched in his white shirt, red suspenders, and matching tie, sartorial holdovers from a previous generation. Each teenaged girl would get a wink and a compliment.

"Mary, you're so pretty, you make my fillings ache," he would say, or some other wonderfully corny remark.

To paraphrase Tolstoy, all small Southern towns have something in common—or so it used to be. Perhaps it still is true, but in a different way. Today these towns have been homogenized into a look reminiscent of a Disney World set. The storefronts have matched scalloped signs stamped with appropriate scrolled designs designating them as historic. Shutters, purely decorative, color coordinate with benches which no one sits on. Tidy terracotta pots hold manicured boxwoods or flowering hibiscus. The Boredwell pavilion is empty, the fountain gone, the spring sealed over with concrete. The tables and chairs and the seedy domino players are also gone. Grass now grows where the playground equipment once stood over bare ground next to the courthouse.

The street behind the stores, a dusty unpaved alleyway called Dog Street in the not-too-distant past is paved now, transformed by boutiques and renamed the more acceptable Dogwood Street.

Language too, like our small towns, is being modified, cleaned up, and moved to mainstream America, free of Southern idiom. Classes are available for those who wish or need to eradicate from their speech those languid, honeyed sounds of their region of the South. Words and expressions familiar in my childhood are heard rarely if at all today. "Dragonflies" darting in the summer heat were called "darning needles" by my mother's generation. "Cape jasmine" is now more often recognized by the familiar name "gardenia." And who remembers that "bachelor's buttons" were once called "raggedy robins"? The effective name "polecat" replaced by the more pedestrian "skunk," seems a loss, especially as an epithet hurled at an opponent. Nothing was more satisfying than calling your enemy a "lowdown, yellow-bellied polecat."

A favorite expression of mine was the name for the humble valise, made of cardboard, its paper surface printed to simulate a textured and strapped piece of luggage which in Sumter County was called a "please don't rain" for obvious reasons.

Perhaps we should resist this homogenization to some degree and join the move toward celebrating our unique character. Perhaps we should start with our own families. I'll write my children tonight to ask if they know what a croaker sack* is.

---

*Croaker sack in some parts is called a tow sack or burlap sack.

South in the Mouth

Lenny Bruce once said that if Albert Einstein had been from Alabama, he never would have been taken seriously. Can you imagine, he said, $E = MC^2$ spoken in an Alabama drawl? He may have had a point; then again, he may not.

So to all of you benighted souls with an accent—more specifically, a Southern accent—there is help available for you despite the fact that you may not have even known that you needed help.

Those one-syllable words you pronounce as two syllables? There is a cure for that affliction. According to an AP release, the University of Memphis is now offering noncredit courses for people in sales, public speaking, or other jobs requiring telephone work or dealing with people outside the South. Dr. Charles Hadley, an English professor at Queens College in Charlotte, teaches similar classes. He also works with actors in roles which require a Southern accent. His most famous pupil was Vivian Leigh, whom he tutored for *A Streetcar Named Desire* to shape Leigh's English accent to the Mississippi tones of Blanche DuBois. Hadley's students listen to voices with no discernible accents to eradicate traces of the Southern drawl which impede their progress in the business world. I find this all very sad and depressing indeed.

I hate to think that those individual tones so distinctive might be eradicated and replaced by the inflection-free copies of the media voices. It's curious to think that you can go to school to flatten your voice into the same uniform mold as that of most reporters. Meanwhile the commercial world is seeking out distinctive voices like Lauren Bacall's for Fancy Feast cat food voice-overs.

The article goes on to say that one student complained that

6

his Tennessee accent was keeping him down in his career as an engineer. He hopes the classes will help in his business dealings with people in other parts of the country, particularly those who equate a Southern dialect with ignorance or slothfulness. Again, I find this a sad commentary on individuality. But I do understand the young man's thinking.

Liz Smith, the Texas-born gossip columnist, says that she finds that her Southern accent does make a difference in her work, but that it is a definite advantage. Her contention is that people are more likely to open their secrets and hearts to you if you have a Southern accent. I don't know what her rationale is. Is the Southerner perceived as a more benevolent listener, more sympathetic, or just less able to remember what you said and therefore less likely to repeat the tidbit?

Personally, I have found the accent to be a real talisman, especially when traveling north of the Mason-Dixon Line, New York in particular. I lived there for a year and a half and found the accent my most useful skill then and now. Everyone is always exceedingly kind and generous to one who sounds like me. It's quite miraculous. The listeners automatically assume that I am either backward, ignorant, or fell from a passing collard truck on Lexington Avenue and am unable to manage on my own. They are unfailingly solicitous and helpful. Willing to play the part to the hilt, I try not to go over the top and drool or do anything excessive, but the accent becomes even more "Alabama" than usual.

Of course, there is no such thing as one Southern accent. There are hundreds of variations on the theme and what fun they are. My husband from Goldsboro says peé-can and my Alabama roots dictate pee-khán. And I'm the only one in the family who thinks that Graham is a two-syllable word.

The Southern idiom is a vital part of the accent viewed holistically. Expressions such as "and how's your Mama?" and "ugly as a mud fence" are as Southern and as pervasive as kudzu. One tag line that can give you plenty of latitude when speaking disparagingly of someone: "Cousin Kitty, why, she doesn't have the sense God gave a baboon, *bless her heart.*" Thus, the rudest remark becomes socially acceptable with that tag-on ending, "*bless her heart.*"

The Southern accent has become a recognition factor for me since I started my commentaries on WHQR. I have no plans to eradicate the accent. I would just as soon go in for a gender change. And, at my age, the accent sure beats a tattoo for that "mark of distinction."

Stamping White Horses and Keeping Cats

In this age of the victim, we are all deemed victims in one way or another. This is an unfortunate trend that surely should be avoided when possible. I don't feel particularly victimized in most aspects of my life but sometimes I catch strange looks, rolled eyes, and raised eyebrows which lead me to realize that I am a victim of my own upbringing in the field of superstitions. My claim is that though we are almost all used to some form of ritual we learned in childhood—whether it is avoiding cracks in the sidewalk to keep our mothers safe or pitching salt over our left shoulders—some of us are infused with less known and almost extinct beliefs closer to the primitive.

I'm talking about those more exotic variations of regional superstitions, which, like our wildlife displaced by urban sprawl, have been replaced by homogeneous cultural beliefs like knocking on wood. This is not to say that there are not perfectly fine superstitions in North Dakota or New Mexico . . . they just aren't *my* superstitions.

Like accents in our speaking voices, our superstitions reflect our roots, and mine lie in those dark regions known as the Deep South. Harper Lee's Boo Radley, Tennessee Williams' Birdie Tutwiler, Faulkner's Emily Grierson, and their real-life counterparts inhabit that corner of the South. Friends may shake their heads, bewildered or amused, but they generally accept these quirks just as they would brown eyes or straight hair. It's just part of the package.

One very practical and reliable superstition you might find useful is on how to keep a cat from straying when you move into a new home—that is, if, indeed, you do want to keep the cat. You must first butter the bottom of his paws. Lather a generous portion of Land O' Lakes (margarine or butter substitutes simply will not do) on the pads of all four paws. Then snip the last half-inch of the hair from the end of the cat's tail and bury those hairs under the back steps. Back steps are essential to the strength of the spell. Sliding patio doorsteps are not acceptable. A friend of mine used *I Can't Believe It's Not Butter* on her calico right after she moved and no one has seen hide nor hair of BoBo since. (BoBo is the cat, not the friend.)

Another essential superstition will help maintain friendship and relatives. Whenever you give a knife or scissors as a gift, you *must* include a penny or some money with the gift. The recipient then gives the money back to the giver. The purpose of this exchange? It keeps the knife or scissors from "cutting the love" between the two. The money exchange assures friendship and goodwill between the giver and the giftee. This superstition might be a distant cousin of the one in *Gone with the Wind*. It was Prissy (the unforgettable Butterfly McQueen) who placed a knife under the birthing bed and explained that it was to "cut the pain" when Melanie Wilkes had her baby.

On New Year's Day, thousands of superstitious Southerners eat the traditional black-eyed peas and collards with hog jowls to assure a fortune in the coming new year. The fare may vary somewhat from one part of the South to another, but the basic peas and greens stay the same. Hoppin' John is the South Carolina version, where the entrée of black-eyed peas is cradled in rice with the greens on the side. In any form, the food means the same. The peas are for an abundance of good luck and the collards are so you will have plenty of "greenbacks." Prosperity and luck make the dish a *must* every January on every Southern table.

One ritual which always brings back my childhood is the stamping of white horses. This is to be done whenever you see a white horse. Multiple sightings mean multiple stamps. A horse is "stamped" by licking your right index finger, touching the moist finger to the center of your left palm, then stamping the moist spot with the heel of your fist with a nice, strong thump. And the meaning? A windfall of good luck with each sighting and stamping. I must have stamped a gazillion white horses over the decades, riding past pastures and fields. And am I lucky? Well, just think what might have happened if I hadn't been stamping them.

Advice from Mama

A new literary genre has sprung up lately and is now appearing in a bookstore near you. Sections called "Gift Books" display numerous nonbooks which bear attractive covers and earnest titles like *Life's Little Instruction Book* and *P.S. I Love You.* These nonbooks feature one thought or aphorism per page. The idea, I suppose, is to keep the book on hand as one would a bottle of aspirin. The direction might read "Adult dosage: Two aphorisms per day. Repeat as necessary." The puzzling thing about *Things My Mother Told Me,* a recent addition to the gift book repertoire, is that the homilies offered are so very different from the bits of wit and wisdom given by my own mama.

An eccentric mama is a necessity if you really want to be Southern. Then you are equipped to tell "mama" stories. Perhaps it's a regional thing. Perhaps mothers in the South are more prosaic or more esoteric than those in other sections of the country. My mother's admonitions were always spiked with overtones of unspoken peril that lurked abroad, pitfalls to avoid along the rocky road of life. "Don't eat strangers' chicken salad" is one I recall. By "strangers" she meant any restaurant cook and even some of her friends' versions of the luncheon favorite. I guess it sprang from the fact that in Mama's youth of marginal refrigeration and beastly hot Southern summers, mayonnaise left out too long could cause chicken salad sandwiches, with the crusts neatly cut off, to be an iffy proposition and could eliminate a goodly portion of the county in one fell swoop.

Language was another territory fraught with maternal warnings. "Never say stink or darn. Unladylike." All anachronistic in this liberated day and age. We were never allowed to call anyone "common." If someone's behavior did deserve this adjective, we were to say "ordinary" or "tacky," both acceptable in Mama's hierarchy of civility.

Another favorite axiom of mine, which I have yet to see in any booklet of maternal wisdom, is "Better not make that face. It might freeze and you'd be stuck looking like that for the rest of your days." This was the general offhand comment made to the child who, in speechless rage, had resorted to making a gargoyle-like face or stretching her mouth into that of a grotesque at another child . . . usually a sibling. The advice on face-freezing was not taken as gospel, as were other bits of guidance —like chicken salad warnings—but did serve to end escalating exchanges between us children.

Other watchwords of advice also fell under quasi-medical headings. "Don't use roll-on deodorant." This in the fifties, when deodorant packaging moved from messy creams in jars into the space-age technology of the roll-on. This seemed to be a basic caution against newfangled ideas which might, in the long run, prove harmful. Perhaps a dread disease of the armpits. Mum was the cream of choice, an iridescent, glistening, salve-like substance which never really absorbed into the skin and left powdery white rings under the arms of your best black sleeveless linen sheath.

One bit of wisdom may ring a bell with many women. (Somehow I doubt that male children were instructed on this topic.) Always wear clean underwear in good repair. No holes, torn lace, or unstitched elastic was acceptable. The reason for this axiom was a very serious medical concern: If you were in an automobile accident and the ambulance driver came to pick up your bleeding, unconscious body and saw torn lace on your underpants, he would refuse to put you on the stretcher. You would be left lying near some ditch on the side of the road, while others with underwear in acceptable condition and good repair would be swiftly transported to the hospital for life-saving care and treatment.

Others I have talked with have said their underwear advice stemmed from social sensitivity. Their mothers insisted that raggedy underwear would be a social disgrace and reflect badly on the family. Shame and embarrassment would fall on the wearer and the wearer's parents. Not in my family. It was *literally* a matter of life and death.

I wish Mama had written a book on her advice. It would have made a killing.

All God's Chillun

A common denominator between all children is their fascination with new shoes. Perhaps it's because shoes are so visible dangling from their legs that the shoes seem to take on a life of their own, independent of the owner of the feet. Some of us never get over this passion. My daughter has a devotion to shoes that extends beyond the boundary of the shoe itself. While some notice the eyes or smiles of the people they meet, she notices their shoes and categorizes people accordingly. It is a threatening position to those who know her yardstick. I sometimes catch myself tucking my own scuffed shoes under my chair to avoid her critical eye. I would hate to flunk the "shoe test" and perhaps risk being drummed out of the motherhood corps because of unacceptable footwear.

Shoes have always taken a beating at my hands (or feet, if you will). As a child during WWII, rationing of shoes was a real hardship for a child known to be "hard on shoes."

In second grade, my mother took me to the shoe store, her woven ration coupon book clutched in her hand. She explained to the shoe clerk that I was rapidly using up the coupons for a family of four because my shoes were always worn and torn beyond repair. Could he please recommend something very durable for a seven-year-old shoe scuffer?

The salesman nodded knowingly. "I have just the ticket," he said.

Disappearing behind the mauve curtain, he returned shortly with a pair of shoes atop his upturned palms.

"These, madam, should do the trick," he smiled.

I gazed solemnly at the ugliest pair of brown oxford lace-up shoes I had ever seen. They looked like boys' shoes . . . boys on their way to reform school for elementary-age miscreants.

"They're Buster Browns," he said, "and this sharkskin wing tip is guaranteed to last for the life of the shoe."

I wondered how many years a shoe lived. What was the life of a shoe? I stared down at the homely face of the sailor-capped boy with his dog Tige on the labels on the instep of the hideous shoe.

"They're boys' shoes," I protested as they were laced onto my feet.

"No matter," Mama brushed my objections aside. "These will last for the duration," she announced.

I was led to the fluoroscope machine to view my feet, to determine if the size were right. This was always the highlight of any visit to the shoe store. (These were innocent days, of course, before we knew that we were happily shooting cumulative X-rays into the feet of every American child.) I wiggled my toes and looked into the periscope-like viewer and smiled at my skeleton bones squirming in the ghostly light. I momentarily forgot the unfortunate appearance of my everlasting shoes.

The shoe salesman proved to be a prophet. The new oxfords were virtually indestructible. When I rode my bicycle, I dragged my sharkskin toes across the rough road surface to stop my bike instead of applying the brakes. The shoes showed no hint of abuse.

Crossing mud puddles, kicking rocks, dragging my feet along gravel paths, my daily mission was to destroy the despised footwear. Nothing worked.

When I *finally* outgrew the oxfords, they literally looked as good as new. I happily packed them in a box to send off to the missionaries in China with wicked thoughts of some other miserable recipient living with the hated shoes, marching along the Great Wall of China trying to scuff those sharkskin tips or slogging through rice paddies in hope of weakening the everlasting last or dissolving the iron stitching which held the shoes firmly in place.

The Transplant

It has been decades since I celebrated Father's Day with my own father. He died shortly after I graduated from college and never knew that I married, have two children, one granddaughter—or anything of my life as a real adult. But each Father's Day, as well as a million other times a year, I reflect on the remarkable man who was such a part of who I am today.

Like so many daughters of the South, I called my father Daddy—never Dad, Papa, or Pa. He was a Southerner by choice, though if you had met him, you never would have guessed that he was a native of Lancaster, Pennsylvania, rather than Lancaster, South Carolina. He had come to the South in the twenties as a young forester, fresh from what would later become the school of forestry at Penn State, to begin experimental replanting in Sumter County, Alabama. He met my mother there and fell in love with her—and her enormous sprawling Southern tribe of brothers, sisters, aunts, uncles, and varying degrees of cousins who were once or twice removed and sometimes even double first cousins. (The true test of any good Southerner is if he understands the fine nuances of cousin removal.) It was a twist on the biblical story of Ruth. Mama's people became his people. For their part, there was never any doubt that he was family.

Our family is full of stories—family stories that are mostly true but sometimes more apocryphal than literal. When my father asked for my mother's hand in marriage, he got the go-ahead from her father but endured a rather dicey confrontation with my grandfather McConnell, a dead ringer, according to old photographs, for Colonel Sanders . . . white linen suit, string tie, and all. Granddaddy allowed that this young man was a forester and nobody in 1927 really knew what that was. Even worse, he was a Yankee and everybody in Sumter County knew exactly what *that* was. After much conversation and negotiation, it was concluded that since this young man was also a Democrat and a Presbyterian, those qualities offset the unfortunate aspects of being a forester and a Yankee. The marriage proceeded with the blessing of all of the family. I might not be here today if Daddy had been a Republican, Libertarian, or Congregationalist.

There were only two daughters in our family, no sons, so Daddy took us exploring in the woods where we learned the names of all the trees, wildflowers, and mushrooms. He was an expert woodsman and naturalist; Thoreau and *Bartram's Travels* were part and parcel of our growing up.

Every Sunday afternoon, we went on an outing to some nearby forest area. We cleverly called our group the Sunday Afternoon Hiking Club. It wasn't until I was grown that I realized that our adventures were in part motivated by Mama's request for Sunday afternoon naps as well as the lure of the great outdoors. We girls, dressed in sturdy corduroy, loved those rugged afternoons of hiking through woody glades, over noisy brooks, and up rocky inclines until we found just the right site for our late-afternoon feast. We would unpack the strange combination of cans and packages: saltines, pork and beans, and Vienna sausages, the pork and beans eaten right out of the can. I can tell you that the finest gourmet foods could not touch those cold canned delicacies on long afternoons when the three of us sat and talked about the bobwhite calls trilling in the distance, spitting on and shining the smooth pebbles from the stream we had crossed earlier in the day and nibbling on the wild blackberries from the fence along the road, our faces deep purple and blue from the sweet juices running down our chins.

Seldom a day goes by that the moan of screech owls at dusk, a box turtle ambling across hot pavement, or the memory of those long-ago Sunday afternoons does not pass through my mind like a clear fresh gust from the underbrush of the sweetshrubs and sassafras.

"Ladies . . . Gentlemen . . . and Children of All Ages"

My father was born in the days of ballyhoo, hoopla, and celebrity, freshly minted from the fertile mind of showman Phineas Taylor Barnum. He used to tell us of seeing the great magician, Harry Houdini, at the Hippodrome in New York back in the early days of the century and what some think was his most amazing trick: a 10,000 lb. elephant disappearing on stage without a trace—right before the incredulous eyes of the audience, who hooted and cheered the feat.

First came Houdini's announcement of the trick, then the murmurs of disbelief moving like a wave through the crowd. Houdini himself led the massive beast onstage, turning him in slow ponderous circles. The walk ended with a trumpeting roar from the elephant's trunk as he raised it to the ceiling of the huge theater. Daddy's retelling had a touch of P.T. Barnum himself in the narrative. Decades after seeing it, Daddy was wowed.

But the circus was my father's real love. His memories of the circus wagons arriving in town, the parade of jugglers, elephants, marching bands, and the three rings in the Big Top itself were retold in detail as high spots of his Pennsylvania boyhood. As children, my sister and I became part of his groupie-like devotion to the Big Top. When the circus came to town, we knew the inevitable predawn ritual was about to begin. Clothes, including coats, hats, leggings, and mittens, were laid out in advance so there would be no dallying in the predawn. You were roused in the middle of the night just like a grown-up to go out on this adventure. Mission: to see the Big Top go up. On those mornings in the frozen blackness, no one else in the whole world but us seemed to be awake.

Bundling up, we headed out in the dark at five o'clock. We

went directly to the train yards at the fairgrounds, where the circus train had already arrived and the giraffes, horses, and elephants were marching Noah-like from the boxcars, down the ramps toward the place where the Big Top was being readied. Through the darkness and the fog rising from the open field, roustabouts pulled the ropes and canvases into place. Masts the size of telephone poles were carried as easily as pick-up sticks by the elephants, which were herded into position. The burly men, their breath coming in cold, smoky puffs, shouted to each other, and to the elephant trainers, until finally the moment arrived when the poles were in place, the electronic winches positioned and the canvases ready.

"On the count of three . . . ready, set, aaaaand . . . up."

The enormous canvas temple rose before us like an apparition from Babylon against the early dawn sky. The Big Top was in place. We all stood and held our breath, awed by its size and its promise in the frozen morning light.

The next stop was the Toddle House, that lunch box-sized, silver dinette that made the best cocoa and scrambled eggs in the world. Seated on the stools with red plastic and chrome tops, we shed our coats and mittens to read the smeared plastic menus. We ate very slowly, hoping to slow down the dawn, which was now peeping through the steamy diner windows, transforming predawn magic to pedestrian daylight.

Years later, home from college on spring break, I found Daddy unaccustomedly forlorn.

"What's the matter?"

"It's the circus. The Ringling Brothers, Barnum and Bailey's Big Top is no more. The last tent performance was last week. We didn't even get to go." He showed me the AP clipping from the local paper.

"It's the end of an era, end of an era," he mourned, shaking his head. Like Houdini and his vanishing elephant, our beloved Big Top had disappeared.

The Centennial Time Traveler

I was stunned to realize that my father would have been a hundred years old several years ago in 1997, had he lived. To think that he was born in the 19th century and his granddaughter was born on the cusp of the 21st century is a startling realization to me. I guess it's like a million dollars. I used to think that a million dollars was an unspeakably enormous amount of money. It does not seem such a huge amount today. So too, a hundred years seems a smaller slice of time than I once thought.

William Faulkner would have been a hundred that year. Frank Capra Sr. too would have been a centenarian. It was a vintage year.

But my father, though not in the history books or literary biographies, was a time traveler of sorts. Not the kind you would find in a sci-fi story, but the sort that made a difference when I was growing up. We were a family of stories—bedtime stories, family stories from generations past, funny stories of things that had happened to one of us that day—told over the supper table or out on the porch after supper.

Daddy had his own brand of stories, action adventures taken straight from the pages of American history. Starring in the leading role as the hero was none other than—you guessed it— Daddy. It would go something like this:

"Well, it was mighty cold that Christmas Eve night and things looked powerful bad for our ragtag continentals that December 1774. Old George (I always called him that) was as nervous as a cat because his soldiers kept asking him, 'General Washington, don't you think we might as well raise that old white flag and surrender? If those Hessian troops don't get us when they cross that river tomorrow and attack us . . . then this miserable weather will do us in for sure.'

'I just don't know *what* to do,' said Washington. 'What do you think, Schaef?' (He always called me Schaef.)

'Well, George,' I said, 'You sure don't want to be remembered as a yellow-bellied coward, whining in fear of those hired guns across the river. I say attack, and do it now. We've got some boats here. Those Hessians must be dead drunk by now swilling down their Christmas grog. Let's go.'"

Here Old George nodded in agreement with Daddy, who shouted the order to the soldiers. So the Americans jumped in the boats tied right there on the riverbank. In the midnight darkness, they crossed the frozen Delaware River, jammed with giant chunks of ice. But Washington was a vain man and, despite Daddy's warning, insisted on standing up in the bow of the boat, since Old George had seen one of his soldiers sketching the general on a scrap piece of paper.'

"George, you ___ fool, sit down." (Daddy always used an expletive here.) "You can't stand up in a boat."

And sure enough, as the small boat beached onto the shore, Washington fell head-over-teakettle and knocked himself clean out. Unconscious.

And who had to lead the troops on to victory against the Hessians and change the course of the Revolutionary War? That's right. My always-modest father confided that from that day forward, old George was known as a heck of a soldier, though a pretty sorry excuse for a sailor.

Daddy gave me a legacy . . . a joy of words and a rollicking sense of history. Though a Pennsylvanian, he had a Southerner's love of language. And best of all, he was a storyteller.

My father left me a rich lode of family memory and imaginative history more vivid and immediate than anything on today's big screen. Perhaps we could call it the "father lode."

Eclectic Eccentrics

I've been pondering lately on eccentrics or, more specifically, what makes a person eligible to be designated eccentric. In the South, almost every family has an eccentric. Larger families may have a score or so of them sprinkled over several generations. In an old TV episode of "Designing Women," Julia declared that in the North they try to hide their peculiar relatives, and to put them away, whereas in the South we are downright proud of them and trot them out into the parlor and show them off as treasures. That's true.

Many of my family eccentrics seem to be women, although they have no corner on the market. Miss Faust, a tiny old lady in Livingston, Alabama, was the only person in Sumter County to subscribe to *Time* magazine, a suspect publication in those parts because of its reputation for liberal leanings. She was often asked about this treasonous subscription (since everybody in this tiny town, with all mail picked up from post office boxes, knew everybody else's business).

"I take *Time* magazine," she used to say, squinting her schoolmarm eyes, "because I like to know what the enemy is up to."

My great aunt, a well-known coffee fanatic and fervent Episcopalian, gave up her beloved drink in an ill-advised moment of sacrifice during Lent one year. Her brother went by to see her and couldn't find her as he went from room to room. Hearing a muffled voice, he opened the closet door in her bedroom and found her sitting on the closet floor, calmly drinking a cup of coffee.

"Sister," he said, "don't you know the Lord can see you drinking that coffee in the closet? Even with the door closed?"

"Of course He can," she hissed, "but the neighbors can't."

My sister has a friend from Georgia who won't eat any food

that moves. A bowl of jello or tomato aspic on the table sends her into eye tics and vapors which do not subside until the offending kinetic food is whisked from sight or she bolts from the table.

My friend Jane is an eccentric-in-training. When she gets her recurring sinus infection, she takes her dog's antibiotic; she started doing this after she noticed that the name and the dosage of the antibiotic were the same. She has not hit the heartworm pills to date.

My husband has a niece who will not eat anything that has a face. Needless to say, she became a vegetarian at age seven.

Some places breed eccentrics like local flora. Chapel Hill is such a place. When an overpopulation of beavers wreaked havoc on a neighborhood pond, the locals considered beaver vasectomies as a solution to the problem. My favorite sight on Franklin Street is the car which has hundreds of dolls' heads epoxied onto the hood and to the top of the car. It's like something out of Flannery O'Connor.

Speaking of Flannery O'Connor, this noted Southern writer sewed clothes in her home economics class for her pet bantam hen when she was a high school student in Georgia. Later, she kept peacocks on her Milledgeville lawn, apparently clad only in their birthday suits.

Right here in Wilmington, North Carolina, we have had, and continue to have, a healthy crop of eccentrics. The artist Miss Elizabeth Chant influenced the artistic community for years. Coming from Milwaukee in the twenties, she set up her studio downtown and took in art students to provide income. Wilmington parents sent their children, young Claude Howell among them, for lessons from the exotic woman who claimed to be a Druid and dressed accordingly. Her long chestnut hair was braided and coiled Princess Leia–style over each ear. Claude (who was later to become a well-known artist himself and a noted and much-beloved eccentric in his senior years) always said she was the ugliest woman he ever saw.

But apparently Miss Chant, who had taken up with a violin

teacher, had a healthy dose of what we used to call self-confidence but we now know as self-esteem. When one of her students did an exceptional drawing, Claude reports, she would let down her hair as a reward for artistic excellence.

So the difference between a character and an eccentric may be simply a matter of degree; "she's a real character," they will say. This is a good sign that with careful cultivation, she will blossom into an eccentric. It's a position or status I have long aspired to. Of course, I know it takes a lot of hard work to make the cut between "character" and full-blown "eccentric." But I'm willing to put forth the effort it will require.

By the time I get to be seventy-five, I hope to be a full-fledged, card-carrying eccentric. Friends tell me not to worry; I am well on my way.

Child of WWII

In the forties, the war effort had galvanized Americans into a concerted effort on the home front to win the war, the last patriotic war where American morale was united and committed to a single goal. But I haven't seen any material depicting the war years as seen through the eyes of the American child. Many of us, too young to be a serious part of this adult drama of the forties, have indelible memories peculiar to the American child of war—a knee-high view, if you will.

In grammar school, days were permeated with signs of the war effort. We bought war bond stamps with our nickels and dimes, pasting them into a book much like the old S&H Green Stamp booklets, redeemable for a war bond. I still have an ancient tin Red Cross button with a folding tab acquired early on before tin was rationed. During air raid drills classes filed into the halls, each pupil squatting against the walls, huddled under our raised arms, waiting for the "all clear" bell.

Scrap metal drives were an ongoing project, and after we had cleaned out our houses of discarded pots, pans, and bikes, we children combed our neighborhood and knocked on doors to collect even more of the prized scrap. The scrap was carefully weighed at the school and carted away by a truck to a mysterious melting destination, which was top secret. We relished the prospect that our old bike might be part of a bomb or a cannon to help the Allies. We had no thought of the eventual destination or purpose of these weapons. We loved the drama, the togetherness of our children's war effort.

At home, rationing had all but eliminated butter, meat, sugar, chocolate, new shoes, and gasoline for joy rides. We used a margarine which came in small white loaves like lard. It was my job to mix the enclosed packet of orange powder into the margarine to make it yellow, and to mold the substance into ersatz butter. It was a job I loved, a chance to squish the white brick of margarine between my fingers with great enthusiasm. Ration coupon books and "meatless Tuesdays" were as much a way of life as cutting the top and bottom from tin cans, removing the label, and smashing them flat.

The war affected games we played. My sister and I dug a subterranean bomb shelter in our backyard and covered the labyrinth of tunnels with boards and scraps of roofing. We played "air raid" with the Hines' brothers from next door and even had a plasma station for the wounded. We manufactured our own plasma by soaking red crepe paper in water and bottling the crimson liquid in glass bottles pinched from the kitchen.

Today the remembrance of those war years comes flooding back when I think of the curious idioms that became a permanent part of my vocabulary. To indicate an open-ended period of time I still say "for the duration." "Victory garden" is a name I apply to all vegetable patches. "A slip of the lip" cautions the hearer to be close-mouthed, though there is no danger of the "could sink a ship" as the original phrase indicated.

I'm glad I was a tiny part of that historic time, when the home front worked in unison to end that last world war. A footnote to "The Greatest Generation." And looking at the heartwrenching pictures of suffering children in Bosnia makes me glad, too, that the home front of the forties was all the war I knew as a child.

Southern Sisters

Sisters have certainly been in the media limelight lately . . . journals of letters to and from sisters, coffee table books of gauzy pictures of famous sisters. In the 19th century, sisters—and in particular, Alcott's March sisters—came into their own as subjects for literature. Those plucky New England March sisters (now there's a 19th century word for you, plucky) who first appeared in the 1868 publication of *Little Women* charmed and intrigued readers then and now. The autobiographical aspects of the book are well known, and the circumstances of the family of women struggling through the trying years of the Civil War reflect that peculiar resilience and no-nonsense approach women have taken whenever hard time, are upon them.

Our favorite Alcott sister is always Jo, outspoken to the point of rudeness, decidedly plain by her own admission, a thinly veiled portrait of the author herself, who despairs of her clumsy, tomboy ways and the misfortunes of her large nose. Curiously, none of the movie "Jo's"—neither Katherine Hepburn in the '30s nor June Allyson in the '50s, and certainly not she of the petite proboscis, Wynona Ryder, the most recent Jo—has a nose remotely like the fictional character's, or the one in the daguerreotype likeness of Alcott herself. Louisa May would probably have been both amazed and gratified at Central Casting's version of her heroine.

But Southern sisters are arguably different from those in chillier climes and have unique qualities of their own. My mother had five sisters, a diverse and quirky bunch of women, raised in Livingston, Alabama, who could qualify as genuine eccentrics on a minor scale. They were known by their maiden name as the "Young" girls in Livingston, but even today the name fits.

As a child, I loved being around these bright, verbal laughing women. They always came back to Alabama during the summers and they sat for hours on end on the gallery that stretched across the whole front of Grandmother's un-air-conditioned Carpenter Gothic-style house. Long after the children had gone to bed and the husbands had wandered back into the house, the sisters sat in their white cotton slips to cool off on those hot languid nights, sprawled in the rocking chairs and glider, laughing, teasing each other, sipping ice tea. Outrageous stories, tales (some wonderfully lurid) about neighbors and friends floated on the summer air, punctuated by giggles and underscored by the night song vibrato of the enormous yellow and black grasshoppers which we children attempted to catch and torment during daylight hours.

If someone drove up into the front grove, car lights bounced across the darkened porch, lit up the oaks around the house, interrupted the stories, and sent the barefooted, slip-covered sisters flying into the house, shrieking and laughing as the screen door slammed behind them. Each scattered to find an "easy-do," as they called any cotton shiftlike dress, to put on for the company.

Making themselves presentable, they returned to the guests on the porch, usually several cousins who declared they "loved to see those Young girls scatter like a bunch of chickens" when the crunch of gravel sounded the alarm to the nocturnal storytellers. The stories continued, but the laughter was never as raucous or as frequent as when the sisters were alone in that special sibling circle.

There were only two children in my family, no rowdy laughing crew like the March sisters or my mother's family. But I always suspected that my sister was very special. She reminded me of her superiority on a daily basis. I found out just how extraordinarily bright she was when I was seven and she, at eleven, was my baby-sitter for one summer afternoon. It was in the '40s and wartime themes dominated the movies. My sister propelled me into the neighborhood movie theater to sit in the cool blackness. We scrunched down in our seats with the thin paper bags of movie popcorn to watch a forgettable wartime tearjerker with heavy propaganda overtones, lost on us children, called *Journey for Margaret* starring Margaret O'Brien and Butch Jenkins.

The plot centered around the plight of a group of orphan children in London during the blitz of World War II. Only one spot was available for one orphan to be airlifted and evacuated to America to live happily ever after. The final choice, naturally, was between Butch and Margaret.

Totally caught up in the melodrama, and sobbing quietly, I leaned forward toward my sister in the darkened theater and sniffed, "Which one do *you* think will get to go?"

"Oh, please," said my sister with great disdain. "The name of the movie *is Journey for Margaret*, you ninny!"

We both turned back to the screen to watch the final frames of the film. But sitting there in the theater, I marveled at her words. It was an epiphany for me. I knew, at that very instant, that my sister was indeed the smartest sister in the entire world.

My Ten Cents' Worth

(Life Lessons from Woolworth's)

First of all, we always called Woolworth's the dime store or the ten-cent store in my part of the world, never the five-and-dime. There is no replacement for this defunct store that figured so prominently in most of our coming-of-age years. The more I think of it, the more I realize that in many ways, Woolworth's witnessed our rite of passage from child to adult in that tawdry, poorly lit sanctum sanctorum where well-oiled dark pine floors creaked and squeaked in a most satisfactory manner and the pungent smell of popcorn and candy permeated our souls.

WOMANHOOD

Initiation into the female world had its seminal explorations at the Woolworth counter. At age twelve, we had the perfect place to try out Revlon's "Fire and Ice" or "Lilac Champagne" nail polish surreptitiously, our eyes darting down the empty aisles to make sure the manager wasn't coming. Every fingernail was lacquered a different shade of crimson. Next, the favorite spot: lipsticks. We drew streak after streak of dragon lady scarlet and hot pink on the backs of our hands to determine the most desirable shade.

After both hands looked as if we might be suffering from blood poisoning, we inevitably settled for the tiny ten-cent tube of Tangee's "Natural," an orangey Vaseline-like lipstick no bigger round than a pencil. We smeared our lips with the glistening orange sheen of Tangee's Natural, the innocuous choice of every thirteen-year-old who thought she was pulling something over on her parents. "Natural" indeed. Real colors like "Certainly

Red" and "Love That Red" would have to wait until we were at least fifteen.

Business and Responsibility

Our dime-store business transactions at age twelve were independently conducted and imminently satisfying to us in our new status as customer. We saved up our allowance to buy the red-eared turtles, cost ten cents, a flattened goldfish bowl, cost twenty cents, and a black pepper–sized box of turtle food which smelled like musty hay, cost ten cents. For under fifty cents, we were in business. The appropriate rocks for the bowl could be gathered from yard or road. The responsibility part was the feeding and changing of water in the small, flat bowl so that the turtle, which by now had its name painted on its back with Mama's fingernail polish, could survive. This was long before the day of the raised consciousness of animal rights, and we took for granted our own rights to mark our turtle, without a thought that we were unlikely to forget its name or that its mark would be unlikely to do the creature any good at all if it escaped into the outside world and onto a nearby street.

Ladies' Luncheon

The Woolworth lunch counter gave us our first taste of ladies' lunch out. The toasted egg salad sandwich was close to haute cuisine at that young age. Sitting at the lunch counter, legs dangling from the chrome stool, and waiting for that cherry coke or the grilled cheese, flat and greasy, was as near grown-up heaven as you could get at age thirteen.

Career Choices

It was in the school supplies section that you could swoon with the fragrance of inks and paper smells and bins bursting with lovely composition books, pencils, erasers, and construction paper. I've often wondered if my going into teaching was not directly connected to my love of Woolworth's school supplies. It was here that I swear my first interest in teaching blossomed. I may not have read that sensory response right. Maybe I was really meant to be a buyer for a school supply chain.

SELFLESSNESS

Even at Christmas, Woolworth's was part of our life preparation. Counters of jewelry, the perfume counter with individual cobalt blue bottles of Evening in Paris or, for the wealthier customer, a gift box of the same fragrance that included dusting powder and cologne in a blue-tasseled flagon, awaited. Decisions, choices, and the final reconciliation of desire and money in hand were valuable exercises for young consumers. Gift selection for family, friends, and teachers nurtured our beginning sprouts of thoughtfulness and a foundation of generosity was established.

Woolworth's holiday counters were filled with decorations, especially icicles, those foil strips now somewhat out of fashion with the Martha Stewart set. Remember the admonition to place each icicle on the tree one at a time, to hang each one vertically? No lobbing a fistful of silver strips at the tree. "They must hang as they do in nature" was the dictum from Mama. And what did this teach us? Patience, of course.

Locations for today's twelve year old to learn the necessities of life as a female are meager and anemic compared with the sensual richness of our dear departed Woolworth's with its unmistakable mystery and character. Somehow, brightly lighted malls and Walmarts have never gotten the smells or lighting right. This next generation is on its own.

Riding the Dog

Sociologists and historians have largely ignored one communication system of the rural South of the '30s, '40s, and '50s. Railroad travel was the most frequent mode of transport to cities, since the poor condition of the roads made automobile travel too adventurous for many. But the obvious limitation was that trains traveled on a fixed route, rarely stopping in small towns like Livingston, Alabama. That long lonesome whistle so familiar to many of us, including our own Thomas Wolfe, indicated the locomotive was chugging and spewing its way to more likely destinations south like Mobile or New Orleans, or north to Birmingham.

Greyhound buses were our lifelines to other areas in nearby counties. We got the gossip and news from the bus drivers: a stop at York would yield tidbits about the recent fire at the First Presbyterian Church (although to be sure, there was no Second Presbyterian Church in that town of 1500 souls). And the fact that Lelia Drayton was standing in the street watching the church fire with her bathrobe on.

In my youth, riding the bus to visit aunts or cousins was a given. We called traveling on the Greyhound "Riding the Dog." These trips provided a breathing spell for our parents and an adventure for us.

Returning from New Orleans to Livingston, Alabama, one steamy August, I sat with two young Mormon missionaries. Immaculate, despite the weather, in white shirts and black ties, they had been sent out to proselytize in the hinterlands of Alabama and Mississippi. Apparently it was too great a distance to make on bikes. As I talked to them, I wondered what was in the kit bags beneath their missionary feet. Beads and trinkets to trade to us natives? I knew, even at that age, if ever there were areas which were in need of the reforming hand of missionaries, it was these two bottom states, Alabama and Mississippi, both teeming with perdition.

Food and the Greyhound went hand in hand back in those days. Sandwiches packed for the trip were usually eaten on board the dog before the bus even left the station. I remember trips with my aunt Marsh, a tiny elegant woman who would carefully unwrap the wax paper from Spartan tuna fish sandwiches with the crusts cut off, sometimes when we were barely out of the city limits. It was a pristine ritual, contrasting dramatically with the life-loving travelers happily slurping their fragrant fried chicken behind us. One family disposed noisily of their shoebox full of fried squirrel and even tossed the bones on the floor of the bus, heedless of my aunt's furrowed brow and pursed lips.

The bus depot right off the courthouse square and across the street from the county jail was a key social spot in Livingston. There the silver Greyhound came through several times a day, disgorging its passengers to rest (translation: hit the bathroom) and eat a meal. The Bus Depot Cafeteria, as it was colorfully named, served real meals: country fried steak, fried chicken, collards, field peas, sweet potatoes, okra, and tomatoes, and cornbread cut in tall hot squares that I still dream about.

The bus was our delivery system, delivering delicacies like the Gulf shrimp that my friend in New Orleans used to pack in ice and ship off in the underbelly of the Greyhound to her landlocked friends in Tennessee, or Hoppin' John for New Year's Eve, shipped from Charleston to a newly married daughter now living in New York.

Livingston, Alabama, like most small Southern towns, prided itself on its ladies' luncheons, receptions, and teas. The usual *pièce de resistance* of these soirées, Black Bottom Pie, a true death by chocolate experience, could only be acquired from Weidman's Restaurant in Meridian, Mississippi, thirty-five miles down the road. You ordered by phone and met the bus to receive your pastries in tidy little white boxes tied with brown twine with your name scrawled across the top, hand-delivered by the smiling Greyhound driver.

I wonder how long it would take a Black Bottom Pie to ride the dog from Meridian, Mississippi, to Wilmington, North Carolina?

Food for Thought

It all started when my friend Marie and I were discussing what to bring to the picnic. I mentioned my marinated vegetable dish and her vegetarian ears right perked up. Her antennae are always out for a good meatless dish. "Sounds like a great side dish. Let me have the recipe."

I began to hem and haw, then confessed that I only had two special recipes in my cooking repertoire and I *never* gave them out. Being a noncook, my culinary "big bangs" are limited. She was horrified that I could be so ungenerous. (Well, let's make that stingy.) I explained that only by marrying into the family could she get this recipe. She reckoned that she didn't see that happening in the near future.

My other secret recipe I call "Livingston Lifecycle Chicken" —named for its place of origin. It is a divine tettrazine concoction of pasta, mushrooms, sharp cheese, onions, other ingredients, and, of course, chicken. This dish is the mainstay of this small Alabama town and makes its appearance at every momentous occasion: the birth of a baby, an engagement shower, a case of the shingles, a bridal luncheon, a heart attack, a broken leg, and, of course, after a funeral at the bereaveds' buffet. Thus the name.

I haven't always been a noncook. My problem may be the fact that I married into a family of excellent cooks, all knowledgeable about the fine nuances of seasonings and spices. I, on the other hand, in my youth took good food for granted and barely realized that its preparation is indeed an art.

I should have known what I was in for in my culinary career. Right before I got married, I asked my grandmother for the recipe for the heavenly Charlotte Russe we always had at Christmas. It was a tradition I wanted to incorporate into my soon-to-be household. Grandmother was a serious woman who had studied at the Sorbonne, taught French at the local college, and could lead a vigorous discussion on Camus and Existentialism, but was less than handy in the kitchen. Betty, an ample black woman with a gift for words and food, was the cook and "assisted" Grandmother in all meal preparation, but she was old and ailing and hadn't been at the house in weeks.

Nevertheless, the delectable dessert was a tour de force, and I knew I could not set up housekeeping without that recipe (or receipt, as it was called). I got my index card and pen.

"It's really easy," she said. "First . . . " I wrote a big number one on the card and waited. She continued, "You go to the refrigerator on the back gallery and look on the second shelf. Take the bowl of custard Betty has put there and then . . . "

I stopped writing. Her voice droned on about the cut glass bowl and the ladyfingers which could be found in the red tin in the safe.

I looked up to see if she were joking. My grandmother was not a jokester. She was not smiling. I continued to write until she finished, gave her a hug and thanked her and left for married life wiser if not endowed with the celestial Charlotte recipe. Let's just say my family enjoyed good food but not necessarily good cooking

I cooked for thirty-four years. Thousands of breakfasts, countless lunches, innumerable suppers. The meals stretched out across the years . . . some eminently forgettable, others actually quite good.

Despite those decades of meal making, my husband's family always said, "Of course, Nan doesn't cook." Eventually, their words became a self-fulfilling prophecy. I *don't* cook any more . . . or very rarely. When I do cook these days, I feel like a bride again. I can't get my timing straight and the dishes come out in assorted degrees of warmth, some even with slightly frozen centers, others burned around the edges.

I despair of ever finding my inner Child—my inner Julia Child, that is. I have called off the search. And if you want to get my two secret recipes, you'll have to come to my funeral. I plan to surprise my friends and have them printed at the bottom of the church program . . . just after the page number of the recessional hymn.

Bread-and-Butter Notes

The day after Christmas is an eerily quiet time. Exhausted relatives have taken to their rooms to read or to nap or to wonder if they can hold out two more days in alien bed and shared bathroom accommodations, the younger set has taken to the malls for the après-Christmas orgy, and the house is so quiet you can hear the fir needles drop from the tree to the carpet below. Without the gifts there, the errant needles don't create that fine sound like rain splattering. It's actually so quiet you can hear the gravy from last night's dinner congeal in the refrigerator—or is that plaque congealing in my own arteries?

In those after-Christmas days of my childhood, the great plague was the dreaded thank-you note. It loomed in the post-Christmas room like Marley's ghost (though certainly less appealing than the Dickens creation), a constant presence only dispelled by the actual writing of the note. And so it looms today.

The custom of writing the bread-and-butter note is still alive and well in the South. The old joke attests to its local vigor. Question: "Why don't Southern girls ever participate in orgies?" Answer: "Too many thank-you notes to write."

The act of writing itself is something I really enjoy, however. The physical act of writing pleases me. There is something infinitely sensual about the long lovely lines of curls and sweeps of the writing and the elegant patterns of blank space around it, like beaches lapped by the tide of the written word.

I must confess to you. I am somewhat vain about my handwriting. At this age and stage in life, my list of vanities is, shall we say, the "short list," so indulge me.

I read recently that handwriting or penmanship is disappearing altogether. Our young are learning to print and then move on to the computer. Somehow, cursive writing is becoming as outdated as the manual typewriter. The old Palmer method some of us learned is disappearing along with the calling card.

And remember the fine Spencerian hand, certainly more elaborate and scrolled than the Palmer hand we practiced so long and hard in those ruled tablets with the solid blue line for the uppercase letters and the broken line for the lowercase letters?

Remember being told not to raise your pencil from the paper on pain of death? What awful fate would strike if the pencil took a deep breath and reared its head for a second or two?

I deal with handwriting every day, some visually appealing, all interesting. My students turn in drafts and journal entries before that final typed manuscript comes in, and I have to tell you that I do peruse the handwriting, making a few mental observations. Some experts say the personality is revealed in penmanship. If this is so, what are we to make of the smiley face O.J. Simpson used to dot his i in his famous "farewell" speech? And will we be relinquishing a valuable tool for learning more about ourselves when everyone communicates by phone or e-mail? Some students cover their papers with large, fat rounded script . . . the letters so enormous that just a few sentences would fill up a page. Others have minute handwriting, reminiscent of the Brontë children's minuscule writing of the *Adventures in Angria*, hand-stitched and bound in tiny books no bigger than your thumb. And, of course, some students, always girls, dot their i's with large, juicy circles or hearts. Are there clues to character and personality there? What do all the slants and loops mean?

Back to my bread-and-butter notes. Perhaps, I think, reaching for my stationery and pen and list of gifts and givers, there *will* be a place for me in the 21st century. An idea whose time has come. Well, not really come but returned. I'll be a scribe, like those in the dark ages when few could write. I start, with a flourish of my pen somewhat like Cyrano's rapier . . . Dear Aunt Adair . . . Thank you so very . . .

Lost and Found

At a book reading some time back, I was reminded of the gothic aspects of much of our Southern Literature, or Grit Lit, as it is called on some campuses. John Shelton Reed recounted the story of a photographer persuading an elderly man from a small Georgia town to have his photograph taken next to his artificial ear. The man apparently had left the ear in the glove compartment of his car, it being a very hot day, and had to scurry out to retrieve it in order to oblige the cameraman. The photograph showed the old gentleman with smiling face and extended finger pointing proudly to his artificial ear . . . on the filling station counter. The idea of an artificial ear strikes me as only mildly odd and unusual.

In seventh grade in a small South Carolina town, I sat behind Nettie Jo McDougal, a gangly plain girl who was largely ignored in the highly stratified social structure of our junior high school. Nettie Jo was shy in the extreme but had a perverse streak that would make Madonna sit up and take notice. Nettie Jo would wait until there was a lazy lull in the class activities and Miss Pittman's back was turned to the blackboard to carefully remove her right eye and place it with a great accompanying sigh in the routed pencil slot at the top of the desk. It was always a showstopper.

Thomas Beale, a classmate of Mama's, had no right arm. As a child, I would watch Mr. Beale sideways as he maneuvered into his seersucker jacket, whose right sleeve was tidily and permanently fastened against his coat. Mr. Beale moved with a grace so quick that it was difficult to see just how he slipped the jacket onto his body, with only a deft assist from his teeth. This was fascinating stuff for any nine-year-old spectator. We all speculated on how he tied his shoes or cut a piece of tough steak without his companion hand, always a subject of conjecture with us children. Even more intriguing was the story of the loss of his arm—a cautionary tale we never tired of hearing. As a teenager, he had gone to Meridian in a 1925 roadster. On the return trip (there were tales that a speakeasy had been visited), the boys had taken turns throwing bottles out of the window at Burma Shave signs. The young Mr. Beale was too intent on his aim or his target to notice the speed limit sign close to the shoulder of the road as the car swerved to give his pitch an advantage. The road sign snagged his arm and snatched it clean off, clean they said like a sawmill's blade. It was hard to think of the dignified Mr. Beale ever being that boy caught in surprise in that dreadful, gleeful aim.

My own grandmother was a wonder I could observe at even closer range. A tall remote woman who looked much like her ancestor, James Monroe, she was a Presbyterian sort of person who took her position as a French professor at the local college quite seriously. She had lost her right thumb in a sewing accident on the old pedal Wilcox and Gibbes. The story was that, as she held the blue checkered material too long under the feeder foot, she became distracted (a believable detail, since she had eight children under foot) and pierced her thumb with the vertical needle, sewing the gingham and her thumb simultaneously. A few days later, angry red streaks raced up her arm. Doctor Hunt pronounced it blood poisoning and his intention was to start with the removal of the thumb and to move up with further amputation if the drastic measure did not halt the fatal poisoning. It did and he didn't.

My grandmother's hand was smooth and dimply where the thumb had been years ago—a neat removal that left the mutilated hand looking strangely whole. She never switched to using her left hand, but continued to use her right hand despite the absence of the opposing thumb needed for almost every task. She functioned quite well, serving thin cucumbers and garden tomatoes from the pressed glass bowl and fingering her napkin in a rather stylized ritual of smoothing and folding it with her four right-hand fingers. I was always impressed when I stopped by her classroom and saw her at the blackboard writing in her elegant script the instructions and assignments "en francais" for the next day's class, with a piece of chalk grasped tightly between the first two fingers of the thumbless hand. She seemed so blasé about her clawlike manipulation, so very matter of fact about it. I never stopped being amazed and fascinated by her dexterity, grace, and nonchalance over what I considered, as a child, a grotesque and freakish mutilation.

They say that after WWI, the streets of Europe were filled with the wounded, maimed, and crippled veterans who suffered amputations and deformities as a result of those awful encounters in the ditches and trenches of Germany and France. Somehow, my childhood in the South was also filled with the casualties of more mundane battles with machines and motors and unknown perils that touched the bodies and lives of those bygone figures from my past . . . those walking wounded whose encounters with their own mortality left them less than whole . . . yet curiously whole in their acceptance. This wholeness "with a difference" may account for the magnetic interest of the young child that I was and the adult I am now.

Theatres of the Absurd

As a child, my earliest recollection of the theater—and I'm talking about movie palaces—was of the magnificent Fox Theatre in Atlanta. The Fox held almost 4,000 moviegoers, as opposed to the cramped rectangle of the suburban movie house today, which holds a paltry three hundred souls. In the main lobby two great staircases spiraled up to the loge and dress circle and lobbies with crimson velvet-covered benches overlooking blue-tiled pools filled with live flashing carp. Towering minarets, crenellated walls, and Moorish arches were vaulted by an enormous domed ceiling of twinkling stars, constellations, and moving clouds over the ersatz starry sky above. We craned our necks to watch the clouds drift and float in this sky inside a theater.

The Islamic theme in the interior auditorium was almost overshadowed by the lavish Egyptian designs in the men's and the women's lounges, a result of the long-running craze for everything Egyptian since the 1922 discovery of King Tut's Tomb: Golden tables and thronelike chairs embellished with images of winged scarabs, the goddess Isis and images of King Tut on his throne, his wife bending close as if to whisper in his ear. It astounded the adults but it bewitched us children. To my six-year-old eyes it was like the magic cave on the other side of the rock after Ali Baba whispered "Open Sesame!"

The tremendous organ called the "Mighty Mo" rose mechanically from the floor below the front of the stage, like an emerging Venus bathed in blue spotlights. Organ music engulfed the movie house with tunes of the day such as "Gonna Take a Sentimental Journey" and "Chattanooga Choo Choo," and Mighty Mo's four keyboards and 3,622 pipes accompanied the opening sing-alongs on the screens. The whole audience would sing "A-

Tisket, A-Tasket," following the bouncing ball over the lyrics projected on the screen.

Less pretentious but possibly more unique was the tiny movie theater, no longer standing, in Summerville, South Carolina. It was here, in the early '50s, that my teen infatuation with film kicked in and never really left. The movie house's brick exterior was eminently forgettable but the interior—well, it was something else. The walls, which rose upward into a barrel ceiling, were dark-russet brick. In this stark and forbidding vault, the whole audience was entombed together, waiting for the opening previews and selected shorts.

Even more startling than the giant sarcophagus effect of the walls were the enormous heads of African animals, a taxidermist's handiwork, emerging *from* the walls. Like early special effects, the walls seemed to morph into wild beasts from a safari movie. Long-dead water buffalo with soulful eyes, zebras with spiky manes predating Punk by some thirty years, lions and tigers frozen in silent menace—all loomed obscenely above the heads of the audience. Two dozen of the creatures hung in that theater, somewhat moth-eaten trophies of long-past safaris taken by the big game hunter, who was also the owner of the theater. Perhaps he was too embarrassed to meet the accusing glass eyes of the great pitiful beasts in his home on a daily basis.

We have an opportunity to recapture a bit of our glamorous theater past right here in Wilmington. Do yourself a favor and escape those shoebox theaters and sterile multiplexes. Head for our own Thalian Hall—opened in 1858 and restored to its full glory in 1988—and experience a Cinematique film shown in a truly monumental theater. Now that's a theater!

Hair Piece

I have to laugh when I watch my son's Labrador retriever paddle through the water off Masonboro Sound. Cody is a retriever who doesn't realize that to swim, the swimmer must get wet. She's a good dog in most canine categories. She retrieves well on dry land. But the water? Well, she just hasn't read the manual on the history of the retriever in those icy Newfoundland waters, and watching her paddle, head raised high to maintain a dry head in the warm Intracoastal Waterway, reminds me of my youth.

It is all too reminiscent of my high school friends and me, paddling along in the pool, necks straining upward like sea otters. Our purpose, like Cody's, was to keep our hairdos intact at any cost. I'm not talking about those girls who had naturally curly hair, who rose from the chlorine like seals, shaking their curls and looking as splendid as they did when dry.

We of straight hair were a breed apart, and we knew who we were. We had every kind of curler imaginable: wire curlers with brushes in them, slick magnetic curlers (for the smoothest curl), soft pink foam jobs (designed for the masochist who planned to sleep in her headgear). Most were clearly from the House of Pain Beauty School. For those with long hair, curlers made from Minute Maid concentrate orange juice cans with both ends cut out were kept in place by bobby pins, truly the most bizarre of all hair apparatus.

We were something to behold when curlers were in place all over our heads—youthful apparitions who were likely candidates for alien abduction or, more accurately, alien abductors themselves. Those were the days of Dippity Do, that disgusting heavy gelatinous turquoise mixture guaranteed to plaster those curls into shape, defy gale force winds, and retain an Italian spit curl sculpted against your cheek into the millennium.

This was well before the natural look. God forbid that any of us teenagers look natural. We wanted to look like our favorite movie stars, coiffed within an inch of their lives—hair which could withstand monsoons unruffled, inanimate faces caked with a mask of pancake, false eyelashes sweeping out like some exotic giraffe. We were sure we looked exactly like Gina Lollabrigida.

Once our hair was rolled into those curlers, it was time for the dryer. No wimpy hand-held dryers for the fifties hairdo. The industrial-strength hooded dryer was essential. Those metal-hooded dryers looked much like those pictures of "Old Sparky," as the electric chair in Florida is affectionately called. A portable variation of the stationary dryer had a plastic bubble hood, attached to a hatbox where it lived when it wasn't on your head. The hatbox was a nice touch which lulled you into thinking the Conover models used this device and then packed it into a chic hatbox. Who would be the wiser as you strolled down Fifth Avenue?

Curled, dried, combed, coiffed, who in her right mind would dive into a swimming pool, swim underwater, and effectively destroy three hours' preparation?

That fatalistic destruction does call to mind a parallel to cooking, though. Perhaps a correlation to the cook's feeling of dismay as the family pushes away after Christmas dinner—when only the remains of the carcass and five hours of preparation vanish as quickly as the diners from the table left piled with dishes. When I say, "Give me a minute to put on some lipstick and I'll be ready to go," my daughter always says, "Mom, you are *so* fifties. Only *you* would think you have on makeup when you smear on lipstick," she snorts.

Maybe she's right. I definitely do have fifties hair. I'll have to remember to keep my Dippity Do out of sight when she arrives for a visit.

Azalea Festival 1958

Today in the annual spring Azalea Festival in the port city of Wilmington, North Carolina, the reigning Queen Azalea is likely to be the star of a daytime or nighttime soap opera. The Queen's court is made up of local beauty queens from the vicinity.

But in April 1958, the Azalea Festival was somewhat different from the way it is now. The Azalea Queen that year was Esther Williams, the wholesomely beautiful swimmer-movie star-athlete of a string of highly popular Technicolor extravaganzas. Those teeth, that perfect flower-entwined hair braided atop her head, those breathtaking dives from forty-foot towers into lighted orchid-strewn pools. Well, you only need to have seen one of these movies to retrieve images of this stunning woman. Most girls growing up in the fifties had practiced her famous backstroke and dazzling Ipana smile each summer at local swimming pools.

Esther Williams was Queen Azalea (Number Eleven) and her court at that time was made up of May Queens from campuses all over North Carolina. Duke, Salem, Meredith, Queens, Saint Mary's all had May Queens.

The University of North Carolina at Chapel Hill had no such queen. But they did have a "Beat Dook" Queen, a figure to reign over the über-competitive Duke–Carolina football parade and game every fall. Yes, there was such a title. And it was mine. So I was sent to the Azalea Festival to represent Carolina and hobnob with the movie stars on my first visit to Wilmington.

Each of us in the court was assigned a specific azalea color for her strapless net gown and matching parasol. The material for the dresses was ordered from New York City and was specially dyed. Actual azaleas were packed in Spanish moss and sent to

New York for an exact azalea color match. The results were striking. Billowing net dresses of pale pink, rose, vermilion, lavender, and purple were a knockout when the court clustered at lawn parties for photo opportunities. Of course that phrase did not exist then. Atop the parade float, which slowly rolled through downtown Wilmington, we were a mass of net azaleas.

My azalea color was "Formosa," that deep purplish hue so popular in Wilmington azaleas. The dress and parasol were a perfect match but it was a difficult color to wear. I remember being envious of the Duke participant, a young woman named Liddy Hanford (her destiny for politics as Elizabeth Dole was evident even then), who had been assigned the more flattering azalea shade of "Pride of Mobile."

Our schedule was hectic but fun. The garden party at Orton Plantation was our first appearance. We preened under the ancient oaks like so many peacocks in the antebellum setting. An elegant cocktail party at Ferguson's Ark, a floating restaurant at the foot of Market Street, I remember mainly because it was my first encounter with smoked oysters on toast rounds. I promptly decided the delicacy was the ultimate hors d'oeuvre. Up until that time I thought celery stuffed with pimento cheese was haute cuisine.

Other celebrity guests I remember included John Bromfield (known mainly from a Western TV series *Son of Cochise*) and Scott Brady (who played the supporting villain in numerous "B" movies). One young actor, Andy Griffith, had recently made quite a name for himself. He got on the elevator at the Cape Fear Hotel that first day of the festival. "Anybody here from Chapel Hill?" he said.

I introduced myself to the engaging Mr. Griffith, proud that we shared the same alma mater. We chatted. The other girls on the elevator were pea green with envy that one of the celebrities had actually exchanged more than the usual superficial greeting. During the festival, Mr. Griffith always waved every time he saw me, smiled, and said, "Hey, Carolina!"

The final event of the festival was a huge dance at Lumina,

an oceanside pavilion at Wrightsville Beach. The turn-of-the-century dance floor was spectacular with its enormous revolving balls glittering with mirrored facets. Lights flashed over the polished dance floor.

I even got to see Esther Williams up close in the ladies' room as she peered into the large mirror over the sinks and pressed that perfect hair into place. She wore her hair pinned up with fresh flowers, much as she did in her swimming movies. Her shoulders were incredibly wide, the shoulders of a professional swimmer. Her heavy white satin strapless dress had come unhooked in the back and she asked if I could help her. She was annoyed at her heavy dress, which was difficult to maneuver, and she made no bones about expressing her discomfort. As I hooked her dress, I was amazed at her language. Remember, this was 1958, and the South to boot. The air was blue with words I had only read in books. It was the first time I had ever seen anybody drink gin on the rocks. I was giddy in this heady Hollywood world.

I saw Andy Griffith in a restaurant last Tuesday. One of my luncheon buddies spotted him and pointed him out. I had not seen him in person for four decades. He glanced briefly at us as we left the restaurant and looked away. He didn't say, "Hey, Carolina!"

Off to Seek My Fortune

I recently wrote a recommendation for a student who was applying for a job at the North Carolina Fisheries. It made me think about my first job those eons ago when I graduated from Chapel Hill and decided the Big Apple was the next destination.

I had gotten the job through the recommendation of my student pastor, who had contacted an editor friend in New York in charge of Episcopal Church Publications. Mr. B. needed a personal secretary, which created an opening for me with one minor drawback. I neither type nor take shorthand, which some might consider a bit of a handicap for a personal secretary.

I promptly enrolled that summer after graduation in Lively Business College, a hometown institution which had been turning out secretarial whizzes for decades. I was easily the oldest student in the class; my colleagues were mostly sophomores in high school who all chewed gum as if it were a prerequisite for success in the corporate world. I got myself a pack of Dentyne, a shorthand tablet, and a sharp pencil and began my crash course into the business world.

Unfortunately, crash was the operative word. My untrained fingers strayed over the typewriter keyboard like drunken errant spiders. I could not take my eyes off the keyboard (a major no-no). Gregg shorthand remained a complete mystery, despite (or because of) ancient and modern languages I had taken as an undergraduate. My colleagues blithely rattled off letters on the typewriter, glancing at the hieroglyphics of the Gregg notepad. My only success at Lively Business College was the gum chewing.

This stumble into the business world should have given me pause. Some hint of disaster on the horizon. But no. Ever the optimist, I was off to New York in August with a degree in English and a certificate of attendance in secretarial school, my six weeks course completed. Note the word *completed* rather than mastered. My best typing speed on leaving Lively Business College was sixteen words per minute, my all-time high.

My new boss was disappointed, to say the least. Mr. B. was a Harvard graduate. He ridiculed my accent, then told me to go on and talk in my "real" voice. He dictated a letter directly to me as I sat at the typewriter. It was immediately apparent that this was not an option. He tried standard dictation, which I was to take on my shorthand tablet. Since I never really learned Gregg shorthand, I scribbled very fast notes about the gist of the letter's meaning. After dictating several letters, Mr. B. released me to my cubicle and typewriter to type his letters from the scrawl in an unknown code on my tablet.

You cannot imagine the daily agony of trying to decipher my own labored notes, an agony exceeded only by efforts at the typewriter. I knew nothing of setting margins. I tried to eyeball the spaces. My words per minute dropped to a heart-stopping low of eleven. Errors were so profuse that it took a ream of paper to complete two or three halfway decent letters. As I ripped each flawed paper from the typewriter carriage and wadded it up, I saw a mountain, an Everest, of balled-up paper rise higher and higher in my wastepaper basket. I was drowning in the secretarial pool.

I made four or five surreptitious trips to the ladies' room for each letter written to dispose of the ruined paper and emptied the basket into the trash bin next to the sink. I knew that if Mr. B. ever saw the paper wasted daily, I would never receive a paycheck. I would probably owe *them* money. I was the secretary from Hell.

It was touch and go as to whether Mr. B. would fire me before I could quit. After seven weeks, Mr. B. went to a convention in Florida for a week and I went job hunting.

My next job was not in the business world. My right brain and my ex-boss have been saying, "Thank you, thank you, thank you!" ever since.

A Christmas Memoir in Three Parts

Part I: Before Martha Stewart

Christmas in Alabama in the '40s was quite different from those my own children experienced and light years away from my grandbaby Caroline's.

Christmas during the war years meant Sonja Henie dolls in skating costumes with red polka-dotted net skirts and real ice skates. And Betsy Wetsy dolls, forerunners of those dolls today who do much more than wet. My children never heard of Sonja Henie, but that's the way it is. I never heard of the Smashing Pumpkins until long after they had left the hot celebrity scene.

Your Christmas stocking in those days sagged with oranges and nuts and chewing gum. The orange was an anachronistic holdover from the days of my parents' youth, when an orange was a big deal. I remember, too, those wonderful lead pencils with your name stamped on them. And the lifesaver book with the title "A Sweet Story" on the silver covers. Inside, ten rolls of multiflavored lifesavers.

In that long-ago time there was no Rudolph or Grinch or artificial tree or Fraser fir. And no balsam or northern evergreen. Those magnificent specimens were found only in books; they were as unfamiliar to my childhood reality as the aurora borealis.

The Alabama Christmas tree had to be cedar. It was years before I realized that the hardscrabble cedar was partial to the unforgiving nature of the native lime-streaked soil and was readily available down any road in the county.

Mama always overdid Christmas. It was part of her general belief system. No Greek "all things in moderation" for her; no Puritan restraint but pure unbridled Victorian abundance was her ideal. There simply was no such thing as "TOO MUCH" in

Mama's book. Never too many evergreen garlands, never too many carols, never too many Christmas cards to wish our fellow men "God Bless You and Peace on Earth." Our house was always decorated to a Dickensian fare-ye-well. Every picture and mirror sprouted sprigs of greenery, fragrant and pungent. Every table held candles, antique brass jelly pots full of holly and pyracantha, lush poinsettias (always red please), and bowls of oranges spiked with cloves.

The mantel was a real tour de force and the same year after year: Mama's own creation of a rolling countryside, covered with snow, complete with her version of a New England village with an approaching Santa.

First, the mantelpiece was cleared. A long roll of brand new cotton batting was unrolled the length of the mantel. The batting was then plumped up to make several hills leading to valleys of lumpy cotton snow. On the hills we placed the tiny thin paper houses with tissue-paper windows, all made in prewar Japan. The tiny church had colored tissue to simulate stained glass and a tiny pasteboard bell in the miniature belfry. Stiff snow-covered spruces on little dowels with bases like tinker-toys dotted the hillside and village.

At the bottom of the hill was the pond, created by a round mirror, somehow separated from some ancient dresser set and reborn as a body of water, the glass edges carefully concealed by tufts of cotton, pulled just to overlap.

The three skaters skimming over the mirror pond did *not* bear close examination. Like Blanche DuBois, they needed the illusion of distance and poor lighting. The figures were molded from some papier-mâché mixture, with "Made in Occupied Japan" stamped on the bottom of each of their thick bases. Our decorations spanned years and wars.

One skater held a little white muff and looked very nineteenth century, while the other two looked like refugees from the Dead End Kids. The sartorial disparity never fazed Mama. After all, she was from Alabama and had never even seen an ice skater.

To the right of this bucolic landscape was where the real action took place. Thundering onto the scene lurched a celluloid Santa in his celluloid sleigh and all eight of his celluloid reindeer. Santa waved a tiny politically incorrect whip over the beasts, who were obviously struggling to get airborne. We had had the reindeer for years; they were getting a little long in their tiny teeth. The reindeer with their minuscule silk harnesses were in various stages of decline; some were victims of involuntary amputation as the Christmases rolled by, and had a definite starboard list as they fought to remain upright in the cotton snow on their three good legs. Blitzen had no left antler at all, and some smart aleck had tried a makeshift substitute, an arrangement with toothpicks which made the tiny reindeer resemble a bizarre and unappetizing hors d'oeuvre.

The crescent moon and golden cardboard stars hung overhead on the gilt mirror above the mantel. The final touch . . . a light dusting of Lux flakes over the whole scene. The translucent flakes reflected sparkles of light. It was indeed remarkable.

The season was officially upon us when the stable and nativity figures were unwrapped and carefully arranged on the sheet beneath the decorated tree. The crèche was one instance where Mama's "more is better" policy did *not* serve her well. The stable held the papier-mâché holy family . . . and then some. Mama always liked to add a figure to the scene if she saw one at Woolworth's that she couldn't resist—another wise man with an especially exotic turban or an appealing shepherd carrying a tiny metal crook in one hand while the other shielded his eyes.

One year an argument arose over the Joseph figure. Somehow there was an extra one. Both were solemn, one in grey, looking downward . . . the other in green, gazing at the middle distance. Neither carried any identification . . . no shepherd's crook or rich giftbox of frankincense. Was the grey one looking at the manger or was the one in green looking at Mary? One was an impostor—but which one? The final decision—the contender in the grey was banished to the outer edges of the scene to join the flock of shepherds, and did not return to the stable.

Once set up, the scene was startling. Wise Men—at least a baker's dozen of them, with standing and seated camels—approached from the right, bearing an assortment of gifts. A mob of shepherds, some with crooks, some without, some with lambs slung over their shoulders (like tennis sweaters I always thought), accompanied by sheep standing, grazing, and lambs couchant . . . all crowded in from the left.

On top of the stable was an angel, arms and wings outspread, a tiny banner across its chest, a bemused expression on its face as it overlooked the sight below.

And in the stable amid donkeys, cows, calves, and goats were those whom the Wise Men and shepherds had come to see . . . baby Jesus, Joseph, and two Marys bending toward the baby. One of the Marys had a poorly painted eye . . . the black paint ran down on her left cheek. Mama had been unable to part with the second Mary, despite her more presentable replacement, so the extra woman still stood in the stable, quietly looking on. The scene was overpowering in the sheer numbers of the cast of characters. Mama made Cecil B. DeMille look like a piker.

It was a formidable vision of the biblical drama spread beneath that Christmas cedar . . . the real reason we have this season at all.

The overpowering childhood memory floods my soul every Christmas when I unwrap the nativity figures . . . especially the second Mary, who gathers with all the rest to see in their midst, in the glowing lights . . . the Baby, the Christ child beneath the tree.

PART TWO

Grown Up Southern

Southern Choreography
(Shall We Dance?)

There hasn't been such an influx of Northerners here since what some call "The Recent Unpleasantness" and others term "The War of Northern Aggression." License plates and accents bear witness to the newcomers from Pennsylvania, New York, and New Jersey. They have immersed themselves in the lifestyle of activities in our town—charity organizations, the business community, our museums and theaters.

Now, don't get me wrong. I firmly believe that our new neighbors bring new energy, ideas, and a cash flow that have vitalized and challenged our area. They have brought a cosmopolitan edge to the sleepy Southern community, which sometimes, like a contented cat, sits on its haunches, smiles an inscrutable smile, and lazily blinks its eyes at interlopers.

Gift shops and bookstores stock numerous manuals for Northern newcomers: too-cute books on how to "speak Southern," vocabulary guides, and primers for the particular verbiage of the Southerner, useful for Yankees confused by local idioms. But beyond language, there are rituals and customs which may go undetected or be misunderstood by the newly arrived. Some may accuse the Southerner of insincerity—even worse, deceit—in his social exchanges. This is usually not the Southerner's intention. It is simply his modus operandi, the way he moves through social situations. Northerners may need a bit of tutoring to guide them through what could be a morass of misunderstandings.

"Come to see us, now" is *not* a firm invitation but simply a way to end the conversation. With distances so far in the rural South and travel so difficult, hospitality was essential—as it was and is in many rural settings. You never knew when you, too, would be a traveler and in need of, as Tennessee Williams knew so well, "the kindness of strangers." Insincerity? Well, can we just call it the choreography of the social dance in the Southern culture? Let me explain.

A recent incident made me very aware that not everyone understands the steps in this social pattern peculiar to Southern females. My friend Virginia, new to the area, told me she had tried to give an older woman a much-needed ride to a museum meeting. But the senior citizen had turned her down, saying it was just too much trouble for Virginia and not on her way. She would make other arrangements. Virginia accepted the refusal, but was surprised when the woman did not show at the meeting.

I explained to Virginia what had happened: That she had to ask the older woman three times if she could give her a ride, not just once. Virginia looked puzzled.

"It's true," I said. "You always have to ask three times. After the third time she would have accepted."

It's the choreography of Southern manners, kind of a distant cousin to having to beg someone to let you do them a favor. These patterns and responses are predictable and understood by natives. Virginia has laughed about this, but has since confirmed that you do indeed have to ask three times to get a positive response. Here's how it goes.

Hostess: "We hope you all can come to the party."

Guest: "Oh, yes. Do let me bring something."

Hostess: "Oh, no. I wouldn't think of it."

Guest: "Oh, please. I'd *love* to do it."

Hostess: "Oh, no. Everything is all taken care of. Just bring yourselves."

Guest: (pleading) "Oh, *please* let me bring something."

Hostess: "Well . . . how 'bout if you bring some of those wonderful cheese straws you make?"

And thus, the exchange is finished. The ritual is complete. The dance is over.

Kith and Kin

Not too long ago, my first cousin Crawford, from my maternal side, came through town with a lady friend. We invited them out to eat Chinese at Szechuan 132 Restaurant, since I have permanently stored my chef's hat and no longer cook at all if there is a way humanly possible to avoid it.

At the restaurant table, we were trying to fill in Cud'n Crawford's friend on the various connections of the people we were talking about . . . Cud'n Marcus, Cud'n Mary Emily, Uncle Monroe, Cud'n Joe Mac, and so on. A veil seemed to fall over the friend's eyes. Her spoon of won ton soup stopped, poised in midair for some minutes. I wondered if catatonic seizures ran in *her* family, but it was certainly a question I couldn't politely ask, since we had just met. My husband had long since gotten that familiar glazed look in his eye—actually some thirty years ago—when the family tales went on and on, most as familiar to him as his own heartbeat.

It occurred to me that we had crossed into that rarefied zone known in some Southern families, where not only the territory was more exotic but the language, too, changed.

Calling cousins "cud'n" was only the beginning . . . the threshold, so to speak, of the journey where few outsiders have dared to follow. We advanced to the upper levels of the game's complexity, crossing into the realm of double first cousins and cousin removal.

I don't know if those from outside of the South speak this way, or if it is an inherently Southern idiosyncrasy. I have never seen cousin removal done north or west of the Mason Dixon Line. (Is there a west of the Mason Dixon Line?) Anyway, I only know that I am inordinately proud of my skill in this dialect . . . as vain about it as if I were fluent in Swahili or Croatian or some archaic language. The almost-lost art of removing cousins is a snobbism akin to name-dropping in some circles, and I indulge whenever the opportunity arises.

What am I talking about? Double first cousins abound when brothers marry sisters, doubling the kinship. This is a pattern familiar to most Southern families, a practice apparently common when fresh marriage material was scarce in rural areas. Of course, crude outsiders sometimes make snide and unkind remarks, best not repeated here, about backwoods Southerners. Hollywood's rude view was clearly depicted in the dueling mentalities in *Deliverance*. After all, if there *is* an occasional distant relative who speaks only in monosyllables or is unable to wear sandals because of an unfortunate abundance of toes, it is only whispered about within the bosom of the family.

Now for the more complicated operation, "cousin removal." When brothers or sisters have children, those children are first cousins to each other. Everybody knows that. Those children's children are second cousins to each other, and so on, in subsequent third and fourth generations. A cinch.

But when is someone a cousin once or twice removed or, heaven help us, thrice removed? When you cross the generation lines. One of the first cousin's children is a first cousin once removed from the parent's sibling. The first cousin's sibling's grandchild is her third cousin once removed. Thoroughly confused? Good. I like to think that those who can pull this off with aplomb are few and far between.

At the end of our Chinese meal, we all read our fortunes from the fortune cookies aloud to each other. Crawford's read, "Family is one of life's real blessings."

His friend's fortune cookie read, "You will soon take an unexpected journey." She seemed inordinately pleased.

Mine read, "When you speak in strange tongues, your audience is only yourself."

The Subject of Snow

A Scrooge on the subject of snow? Well, it dates back to a winter some forty years ago when I began my first real job. I taught fourth grade in an Episcopal school up on West 113th Street below Columbia University in Manhattan. Our headmistress, Mother Ruth (or Mother Ruthless as we frequently called her), had old-fashioned beliefs about the relationship between mind and body. All students were to have forty-five minutes of play in the fresh air in the park every day, no matter what the weather.

During those frozen months in varying degrees of fierce winter, my thirty-three students and I daily marched dutifully to Riverside Park overlooking the Hudson River, only a block away from school.

The ritual of suiting up was reminiscent of the astronauts' pre-blast-off preparation. We checked ourselves at every stage of dress to make sure no one had forgotten a vest, sweater, flannel shirt, earmuffs, cap, and additional wool scarf to mummy up the bottom of the face. Now multiply each layer thirty-three times and you have some idea of the magnitude of this class toilette.

Finally we were ready. My last piece of vital equipment was the long length of thick cotton rope, tied in knots at twelve-inch intervals and strongly resembling an instrument from the Inquisition. The rope was essential for the safe crossing of Riverside Drive with my thirty-three charges. As we approached the intersection, I straightened the double line of children who always walked in twos and ran the length of the rope down the center of the double line. Small mittened hands grabbed the rope, one child on each side.

When all the children were attached and the light turned green, we shuffled hastily across the street into Riverside Park.

We were a multicolored millipede with our rope as a backbone: a creature with sixty-six small boots and galoshes. Once safely across, I collected my rope, rolled it into a coil and we all descended into the wilds of the park, which dropped right down to the banks of the Hudson, where great glacial hunks of ice glided southward. Icy blasts from river wind were paralyzing in their intensity.

As the minutes ticked by, our layers of clothing methodically soaked the cold wetness into each layer by degrees. The children played on, uncomplaining and unconscious of the cold. They had been born in this frigid landscape; I had not. When we had satisfied the required time in the healthful outdoors, I blew my whistle in frozen shrills to gather the children, hooked them up to our rope lifeline, and trudged back through the snow to school.

The final assault on my Southern sensibilities was something of a grand finale. We pulled off boots, mittens, scarves, jackets, caps, and mufflers and draped the wet wool in strata on the big silver radiators on either side of the room. As we settled into social studies, clouds of steam rose like smoke signals from the radiators. The mounds of wet wool overwhelmed the senses with a powerful odor akin to that of an enormous wet dog.

The smell intruded into the classroom, seeping under the desks, creeping into the corners with that unmistakable fragrance: Eau de Wet Wool. I can conjure that smell just by the telling of it.

No winter wonderland for me. That lovely snow is so inextricably bound to that suffocating smell in my New York classroom long ago that thirty years on the analysis couch would not free me from the grip of that association.

Cryptic Messages

Have you ever received a message which puzzled you? You re-read the sentences, and still don't understand the meaning? Then the message reveals itself, like those sixth grade slow-motion science films of the birth of a chick (the eggshell suddenly trembles from the pecking inside, cracks, opens a tiny bit, then a larger hole, then the head of the chick, finally the whole chick emerges). After another reading, you grasp the total, the complete meaning of the image or the message.

This kind of epiphany comes to me from time to time and never fails to startle and delight me . . . much like the famous "a-ha" of the science world except, of course, on a less momentous scale. Sometimes the translations of these cryptic messages are laughable, sometimes enlightening; other times, the message remains, like Tantalus' fruit, maddeningly out of reach.

Some weeks ago, during the lunch snarl on Market Street, I saw a huge battered revival tent on an empty lot. The bedraggled grey tent sagged against its slack guy wires. A ragged plywood sign held the message in large clumsily painted letters: THE FINAL DAYS.

Since I was in the middle of research involving fundamentalist religions, I made a mental note to come back and check on the scheduled times of the meetings so I could attend. What luck! Right on Market Street . . . easy to get to, and the focus was obviously on the rapture and the book of Revelation.

When I returned that afternoon, I pulled back the flap of the ancient revival tent and saw, not folding chairs for prayer meeting but what seemed like an acre of barcaloungers . . . blue velvets, beige plushes, and green naugahydes. Rapture, indeed, for those seeking a great deal on recliners rather than religion.

A chance encounter left me puzzling over another cryptic

message whispered to me by a stranger. Leaving a Chapel Hill nursing home after visiting a dear relative, I took a wrong turn and wandered down an unfamiliar passageway looking for the exit. I passed several patients parked alone in wheelchairs against the hall wall.

"Psst . . . " one ancient lady hissed at me. I looked around; I was the only one in the hall.

"Psst . . . " she beckoned me over with a gnarled arthritic hand. I leaned closer to hear what she was saying.

"I know the rules. You have to know the rules of the game here and I know them."

She repeated this over and over until an attendant showed up and rolled her away, still mumbling about her inside tip on the rules of the game. It was a strangely chilling exchange.

I told my sister about the incident. She was appalled that I had left without finding out the rules. "I've been trying to figure out the rules my whole life!" she said.

We still talk about that missed opportunity.

My mama was the source of one of the most cryptic but powerful messages which made little sense to me at the time. The night before I was married, she came to my bedroom, ostensibly to oversee my trousseau packing.

Finally, she said, "Baby, there is one important thing you need to know for a happy married life."

I looked at her sideways, not believing that at this late date I was getting a "Birds and Bees" lecture on marital sex. I'm from the generation when helpful pamphlets and books were discreetly left in my room. No actual conversation ever took place. I waited.

She held my hand. "Baby, never ever iron a man's shirt," she said slowly.

We looked in each others' eyes for what seemed minutes. She got up, straightened her dress, and left the room. The marital pep talk was over.

Needless to say, I was totally bewildered by the advice but I have never forgotten it.

I thought about it during the early days of our marriage as my husband's shirts were dutifully sent out to the laundry, even if it meant eating beanie-weenies for several days running. I continued to think about it when I realized that the application of the meaning extended far beyond ironing a man's shirt. Don't start anything you're not willing to do forever! The message is concise, wise, and universal. Confucius had nothing on Mama.

Aelurophile

There seems to be no middle ground on these creatures. Much like garlic, they are either liked or disliked. A taste for cats is rarely acquired. I know of only one name for those who love cats—aelurophiles. I found five names for those who have a fear or dislike of cats: gatophobe, felinophobe, galeophobe, eulurophobe.

Our family cats have mostly been polydactylic. No, not cousins to the dinosaurs but multifingered (or toed, I guess it would be with cats). Cats similar to Anne Boleyn, with her extra digit on her left hand—whose long sleeves with the flowing backs were actually invented to hide her peculiar appendage. Or one of Hemingway's famous congregation of six-toed cats in Key West.

Our last cat was a polydactyl, and as an adult resembled a Maine Coon cat, though a native of the Old North State. Bullet was from a litter of multitoed kittens nesting in a large Food Lion box bearing a handwritten sign, which from the looks of it may actually have been written by a polydactyl person: "Free Kitties—Many Toes." We were especially taken by one tabby's huge paws and the discovery that, indeed, he did have an extra toe. It was an omen. His polydactyl predecessors had led us to him. He was soon homeward-bound.

Bullet was a terror, flying from place to place with the velocity of a speeding. . . . Well, it does explain the name. Bullet was hell on paws, if you will excuse the expression. He moved as if he were on amphetamines. He was un-languid and un-catlike. This was a cat with a mission or perhaps he was just "possessed" as my son suggested.

As a kitten, Bullet took to tormenting our black lab, Lizzie Borden, a dog with all of the virtues and few of the vices of the breed. Patience was her long suit. Bullet would latch on to the dog's ear or hind leg with tiny teeth and the grip of the jaws of death. Lizzie would amble from place to place with the kitten attached like an oversized pendant earring or furry anklet. This bizarre behavior lasted well into the cat's adolescence, when his sheer size made the hitchhiker give up his abuse.

Something about Bullet—perhaps his name—made you want to talk to him like a character from a Damon Runyon story or a Spillane paperback. Actually, his name and fierce appearance belied his artistic temperament, which developed as he matured. His linguistic preference was French, especially when flavored with a soupçon of south-Alabama accent. Bullet preferred to be called *Monsieur La Bulle* when he was feeling especially imperious.

A natural musician, but not a vocalist, he preferred string instruments. He took to playing the screen door on occasion, plucking away at it as if it were a fine gilt harp. He would then pause, waiting for acknowledgment. If it were not forthcoming, he would sit taller and the twelve toes would pluck even more insistently, an eerie melody. Other times, in a more "down home" mood, he would crawl under the bed, lie on his back and twang away vigorously at the bedsprings, a discordant banjo-like tune, until some Philistine family member would holler for him to "knock it off."

Bullet was a magnificent-looking specimen. His huge ruff circled his mighty head, balanced by a great bushy tail any wild raccoon would trade his mask for. He was first runner-up in the *Wilmington Star-News* Fat Cat Contest one year; a movie star glamour shot of him appeared in the paper.

But Bullet's size became a cause for alarm; he was diagnosed as a diabetic due to his appetite for life and his family's inability to resist his pleas and howls for tidbits from the table. Insulin shots and a Kate Moss diet were required. Bullet learned to be docile, even eager to take the hypodermic needle twice a day, when he realized his meals were both limited and strictly timed to follow his insulin shot.

After three years, the disease got the best of him. He is buried in our backyard under his favorite magnolia tree. Sometimes on warm summer days, I *think* I hear a musical plunking on our screen door, gently at first and then more insistently.

Boo!

Merchants have had those bilious orange Halloween displays out since Labor Day, something I find a bit obscene, along with those early turkey, Pilgrim, and Santa Claus images that are looking shopworn and a bit long in the tooth after four months exposure before the actual event. Remember the good old days, when all the Christmas stuff was only put out the day after Thanksgiving, and nary a Christmas carol was heard in November?

But back to Halloween. I read in a Halloween bit in the newspaper that a proposed law to ban outhouses in Wisconsin was defeated. A citizen's group called POOP—People's Organization for Outhouse Preservation—fought the idea and defeated the proposal. Among their key arguments for preserving outhouses: Outhouses provide Halloween entertainment.

Toppling outhouses used to be the ultimate prank in my mother's childhood in rural Alabama, but was long gone before my lifetime—at least in my own experience. Halloween, along with other holidays, has undergone drastic reinvention in the past decades.

Today, the adult world seems to have stolen Halloween. Restaurants have every waitperson dressed in Halloween costume. Elaborate Halloween cocktail parties and midnight theme dinners are given all over town. Adults spend as much time planning their outfits as they do selecting a wedding dress. Merchants have elevated the day to the commercial pantheon along with Mother's Day and St. Patrick's Day.

But I am old enough to remember when Halloween was strictly for kids, and adults were not allowed to horn in on the fun. As children we wore made up costumes: bathrobes, hats, and sashes gathered from closets and trunks, and all manner of flashy costume jewelry scrounged from Mama's dressing table to transform ourselves into gypsy fortunetellers, pirates, and sheiks. With Daddy's old clothes and hats, and with burnt cork on our cheeks and chins for hobo stubble, we were tramps. The only store-bought items—or "sto bought," as we said—were the masks from Woolworth's with the black elastic band to hold them on your head. They were made of cheesecloth, with some sort of paraffin stiffening in them to hold the shape of the face of the princess or pirate or hobo. I'm sure those masks would make today's fire marshal cringe. The masks always got soggy and nasty around the cheesecloth mouth by the end of the evening with all the hollering you did—not to mention the eating.

One very strange Halloween, an adult neighbor, Walt Keller, came trick or treating with an empty whiskey glass. He had been "treated" at several neighbors' doors before he got to our house and was in the full Halloween spirit (or spirits). We had been debating taking our dog, Freebie, to the Humane Society, since he nipped a neighbor child with great regularity. We were discussing this problem with Walt, our inebriated doorbell ringer, when he said that for one drink, he would take Freebie as his "treat." The exchange was made and Freebie went to live with the Kellers for a whole year. Freebie was returned to us the following year, after he offered to bite a policeman who had stopped in the neighborhood.

When my own son was a toddler, we were invited to a neighborhood children's party and, though he was less than two years old, a costume was mandatory. A friend volunteered a hand-me-down doggie outfit that almost fit and would certainly be fine for a one-hour social occasion. When the time arrived for us to suit up and leave for the party, my little fella let me know that he did not care to participate. He was terrified of the dog costume. Howls of protest greeted my attempts to snap the headgear beneath his chin, which would transform him into a distant cousin of Deputy Dog. Tears, flailing arms, and a full-blown tantrum made it clear that this toddler would not wear this dog costume or any other terrifying regalia. This was definitely one dog that wasn't going to hunt. I decided on the ultimate practical solution and in five minutes we were headed out the door with no tears and a smiling toddler guest.

My son won first prize for best costume. The prize was a huge plastic jack-o-lantern with flashing battery-powered eyes, which he hated, and I loved. Not bad for his first Halloween party. And with no costume. He was happy as a clam in his regular little corduroys and sweatshirt. Unbeknownst to him, he *was* in costume. Pinned to the back of his shirt was a 9 × 12 sign, which read, in big black letters:

BEWARE! WEREWOLF DISGUISED AS SMALL BOY

Scratch and Sniff

L eave it to the Brits to add a truly unique approach to the scratch and sniff repertoire so prevalent in the glossy magazines today. Recently, the Smelly Old History series published by Oxford University Press featured history books with the smell of muck heaps and plague-ridden streets to transport you back to medieval times.

We know that the sense of smell plays a central part in our lives from the very beginning. Scientists tell us that even newborn babies can identify their mothers by smell. Until recently, however, this sense has been the most underrated of our five senses. We somehow believe we have evolved beyond this primal sense; we consider smell second-rate, ranked far below our senses of sight and sound. But appreciation of smell, our atavistic sense, is coming back after a long exile.

While animals build their lives around smell, we act as if it were an optional sense. We do know that in the animal kingdom, pheromones play a crucial role in mating. And while not the case, scientists tell us, among human beings, we know that research proves that 71 percent of all men and women rate smell as a turn-on.

According to studies, women seem to have a better sense of smell than men. I realize the truth of this piece of scientific evidence when my husband emerges from his toilette wafting heavy layers of Brut. Subtlety is definitely not part of his fragrance trousseau. This gender difference could also be observed when the baby's diaper was sending a signal that could be received by a moose four states away, and my husband could blithely outwait me in the showdown as to who would flinch first and change that ripe diaper.

We have all been in those tight aromatic situations when

breathing becomes a hazard to our health. I remember all too well one beastly hot July day in the Sistine Chapel, on tour with my sister and five hundred other tourists, mostly non-American, who did not care to erase every vestige of those fabulous pheromones on that hundred-degree day. As we stood—necks snapped back in the typical Michelangelo chiropractic neck crick, gazing upward—my sister allowed that she, not usually the type given to vapors and fantods, as they say, was overcome. Not by the unwashed Sistine ceiling murals, but by our unwashed fellow travelers.

"I think I'm going to faint," she whispered. Her eyes rolled dramatically in her lolling head.

"Don't you dare," I hissed, hoping my reprimand would dissipate her dilemma, a case of mind over matter. "And even if you did, you couldn't fall down." I knew this to be a fact since we were both wedged solidly into a sardine mass of sweating humanity, and the crushing mass, defying gravity, would not have allowed any object—much less a body—to fall to the floor.

I looked at the surge of bodies crushing us from every side. "Buck up," I said.

She did. Her attack of the vapors passed.

Now the commercial world has discovered what we used to know long ago. Smell is a very big thing. Odors are now touted as mood changers. They perk us up, calm us down, help us lose weight, coax us to buy things, make us feel safe or anxious. Decorators are now using what they call "environmental fragrancing." Fragrances are piped in like elevator music to define the mood. Scientific researchers have found that the scent of vanilla during an MRI makes patients less stressed during the procedure. Researchers record that 25 percent fewer errors were made on a radar screen test when participants sat in a peppermint-scented room. It's enough to make you carry your own protective herbal fix with you like the garlic-wearing Transylvanians. God forbid your health care provider be an anosmic (a two-dollar word for one with an inability to smell.)

It is an anatomical fact that smells travel a path directly into the limbic system, the center of memory and emotion. It is thought that this direct path accounts for the experience of being instantly transported to grandma's kitchen by baking smells or to a family camping trip by the scent of pine needles. New car smell, now sold in aerosol cans, may bring back those days of a love affair with that first Chevy or some adolescent wrestling matches with an eager date.

I never smell fresh-cut grass steaming in the summer sun without a flashback to Grandmother's sleeping porch where we cousins napped in iron beds with chipped white paint. Transport yourself to a time past. Uncork a memory today and let your nose do the walking.

Going Postal

A few years ago, *Newsweek* reported that the U.S. Postal Service had removed all clocks and calendars from thirty P.O. lobbies and labeled those items as "non-user friendly." Spokesperson Sandra Harding said, "Clocks look bureaucratic. They are not part of the post office experience. The idea was to give the P.O. a more streamlined, retail feel which will expedite transactions," she concluded.

So, removal of the clocks is not about decreasing the customers' anxiety as they wait and watch "their lives tick away," but to make the transactions go faster? This is confusing. Wouldn't the ticking clock gently prod everyone, both customer and P.O. worker, to expedite matters? Tempus fugit and all that carpe diem stuff? Long chats at the counter or dawdling over which stamp to buy might be shortened or even eliminated.

No calendars, no clocks? Is that why sometimes it takes only two days for a letter to get from here to the Raleigh-Durham Triangle and other times takes as many as ten? Is the removal of the calendars an effort to obscure the fact that you might be in a line at Christmas or tax time not only for hours but also for days? I think this may be when the term "snail mail" came into the lexicon. And I'm amazed at the role model the P.O. is using. Retail?

I love the verbiage in this news release. It makes you wonder if the postal middle-management folks are trying to break into stand-up comedy. I like to meditate on what the "post office experience" is.

Consider the P.O.'s approach to damaged mail. Today, a letter of mine was returned, chewed into shreds. The mangled envelope appears to be the work of a large rodent. The remains of my letter are hermetically sealed in a plastic bag with a message stamped on its plastic exterior.

The message reads as follows:

Dear Postal Customer
The enclosed has been damaged in handling in the postal serv-
ice. We realize your mail is important to you and you have every
right to expect it to be delivered in good condition. The Postal
Service makes every effort to properly handle the mail entrusted
to it but due to the large volume, occasional damage may occur.

P.O. Translation #1:
We are overwhelmed by the amount of mail we handle. Your
expectations are unrealistic. The error is not our fault.

The message continues:

When a Post Office handles in excess of two million pieces
of mail daily, it is imperative that mechanical methods be
used to ensure prompt delivery of the mails. Damage can
occur if mail is insecurely enveloped or bulky contents are
enclosed. When this occurs and our machinery is jammed,
it often causes damage to other mail that was properly
prepared.

P.O. Translation #2:
While the damage is not the Post Office's fault, it is not the
sender's fault either. It is not our fault; it is not your fault.
Some other irresponsible letter writer used a bulky envelope
or did not seal it properly so we all have to suffer. The error
is not the fault of the Post Office.

I rather like the P.O.'s chutzpah and its cavalier approach. It
eliminates any blame on the sender of the letter or the P.O., despite the obvious fact that the letter left my possession in good
condition and returned a gnarled mess in a see-through body
bag.

The message concludes:

We are constantly striving to improve our processing methods to

assure that an occurrence such as the enclosed can be eliminated.
We appreciate your concern over the handling of your mail and
sincerely regret the inconvenience you have experienced.

P.O. Translation #3:
Don't get on our case. We're doing the best we can. The error is not the fault of the Post Office. Get over it.

I looked at the regurgitated mess in the P.O. baggie and dropped it into the wastebasket. I stood for a minute, gazing at the little postal body bag, and decided to go re-read Eudora Welty's short story, "Why I Live at the P.O.," and contemplate simpler times.

Necessity: The Grandmother of Invention?

I stood looking at the computer desk for some time. The price seemed reasonable. But it looked huge. No info on size on the price and feature card. No one in sight to ask for a yardstick. So, I began to measure with my hand—the width of thumb to third finger—one, two, three, and so on. An older gentleman passing by stopped and asked, "What are you doing?"

"Measuring," I replied.

"And how many feet is it?"

"I haven't a clue," I said, "but it is four handspans deep and eight handspans across."

He chuckled as he walked away.

Men and women have known or figured out alternate solutions to problems for centuries. One woman has even made a business of that can-do attitude. The syndicated newspaper column "Hints from Heloise" gives homespun remedies for nagging little household problems and clever ways to skin the proverbial cat, should you have a need for that. Actually, Heloise isn't the original Heloise at all but her baby-boomer daughter who has taken up Mama's mantle (which is probably a ratty, recycled chenille bedspread), and has an advice column using her mother's title. But this new Heloise lost me several years ago when I read an ill-advised suggestion combining thrift and an inventive use of a product in a way for which it was definitely not designed. The suggestion was for a use for pantyhose with a run in one leg.

Now, we all know the early suggestion that we cut off the leg of the pantyhose with the offending run, find a similar pair with a run, cut that runny leg off, and then wear the pair, which, now that they are combined, have two perfectly good legs. Never mind the double band of elastic wadded and bunched around your waist or the fact that you now have a double crotch to contend with—not to mention a logistics problem Heloise never gave a thought to: negotiating a trip to the ladies' room.

Anyway, my falling out with Heloise the Younger came over her more recent pantyhose hint. She suggested we cut off the good leg of the pantyhose and discard the remainder. Now, that's progress, I thought, reading on. Then we were to rinse out the good stocking leg, put the cottage cheese we were making into it, and drain the excess liquid from our homemade cottage cheese, the pantyhose acting as a strainer.

My automatic gag reflex kicked in and I could read no further. I couldn't decide if I were more repelled at the thought of the pantyhose cottage cheese strainer or the thought of actually making my own cottage cheese. I always thought that those little cartons of cottage cheese grew on small bushes before they were plucked at the height of their ripeness and rushed from the fields directly to the Harris Teeter. I abandoned resourcefulness. I took the oath and swore off Heloise that very day.

But my students have made me fearful that our famous American ingenuity may be in peril. Two days of a research writing class were canceled during a recent hurricane and, of course, we all lost electrical power the weekend that followed. Our research paper was due Monday. Even with the power off, we all had at least fifty-two hours of natural daylight before the next class. Monday afternoon at the beginning of class, I asked for the assigned papers. A silence and a sea of astonished faces—then a long collective groan. Wasn't I aware that we had had a hurricane? Didn't I know the electricity was out, the computers down?

It made me wonder about this X generation, who can handle a computer with the skill of a Paderewski, sing the lyrics to a thousand songs whose words I can't even decipher; they're bright and hip. Yet I have begun to speculate that if Lincoln were alive today, he might have decided to forgo the address at Gettysburg if, when he boarded the train, he realized that Mary Todd had forgotten to pack his laptop, not giving a thought that he *did* have a pencil and old envelope in his pocket.

The Last Roundup

I used to think that orchestrating children's birthday parties was my long suit.

My Martha Stewart juices would rise at the mere thought of a theme party: A magic party, complete with amateur magician, or a roller-skating party with the cake elevated on real roller skates for the après-skating activities. But my daughter's sixth birthday party was something of a tour de force. It was to be the ever popular "movie party," centered around the viewing of the Technicolor horse saga, *Smokey*, showing at the theater downtown. We sent out invitations, a Mister Ed–looking creature saying, "Let's mosey over to the birthday party," and ordered a cake with an impressive chocolate stallion rearing up on his hind legs between the "Happy" and the "Birthday." There was even a split-rail fence around the perimeter of the cake.

The five little guests arrived clad in a variety of cowboy hats, fringe vests, and tiny boots. It looked like a convention of Lilliputian cowgirls. We loaded the station wagon and headed toward the Majestic Theater. I was amazed and horrified to realize three minutes into the movie that *Smokey* was actually a poor man's *Lassie Come Home*, my own personal favorite from childhood. The script had been reworked to substitute Smokey the horse for Lassie the dog, as in Smokey meets boy at village school while the town clock chimes three, Smokey is sold from the family and has endless heartbreaking adventures. Well, you get the idea. Was nothing sacred?

My ruminations on the blasphemy prompted by the unimaginative filmmaker were interrupted by a heart-wrenching sob coming from my cowgirl contingency. I led the sobbing child to the lobby and held her on my lap, assuring her that Smokey would indeed survive and would happily be united with his owner. The outcome and precise plot turns were easy to predict. She was mollified by the reassurances and a box of Raisinets.

The real trouble began when I led the tear-stained group out of the theater and back to the station wagon. Or at least to where the car had been parked. It was gone. No wagon at the curb. I frantically herded the children back into the theater and told the usher (there's a relic from the past) to call the police. "Oh," he said, stepping behind the candy counter to arrange the Bit-O-Honey bars.

"A blue station wagon? Ford? Right out front? The police towed that away." He finished up the candy arrangement and returned to his meditation on his *Archie* comic book. I called my husband. No answer. I looked in my wallet. Four dollars and twenty-three cents. I called a taxi and loaded my semi-hysterical cowpokes into the yellow cab. The children recovered somewhat with the cab ride. None had been in a taxi before, so the meter and the uniformed driver were a thrill.

But the police station was even more exciting. The revived cowgirls scurried off in all directions to explore. I learned the station wagon had been impounded two miles away. The police would have to take me to the place, in the black and white, to retrieve the car. They assigned two patrolmen to corral and watch the little cowgirls while I went for the car.

The police said they were really sorry I had been towed. I think they meant it. They were even sorrier by the time I got back. The patrolmen looked dazed from their baby-sitting duties. The cowgirls were in full roundup mode. We headed home.

They were totally out of control by the time the parents picked them up at the house. The melodramatic tearjerker, the police station/jail tour and semi-incarceration, topped by the chemical sugar high from eating the stallion cake, had rendered the little cowpokes frantic and manic. News of the "jail house party," as the event was referred to by then, spread quickly through the neighborhood and school. There had not been a movie party, cookout, or swimming party that came near it for pure drama. It became the yardstick by which *all* other birthday parties were measured. Let's just say, no other birthday party could hold a candle to it.

Baaa None

On my daughter's sixth birthday party, we wound up at the police station—a colossal disaster or success, depending on the adults' or the children's perspective of a party gone awry. We decided to opt for the bucolic setting for the seventh birthday. Well, bucolic for Charleston anyway. Nearby Middleton Gardens would be perfect for a birthday picnic. It is a working farm, as well as a 17th century historic plantation. On previous visits, my children had loved riding in the haywains and feeding the goats, horses, and other barnyard animals (especially the enormous hog named Bacon, who must have weighed in at nine hundred pounds and sometimes even managed to upright his tremendous bulk and stagger to his feet to greet children who brought yet more edible, non-dietetic treats). The Middleton animals were accustomed to being fed by tourists and visitors.

This was to be a catered affair (Kentucky Fried Chicken had been called) for seven little girls who were instructed to wear farm outfits. The children arrived wearing Old McDonald outfits: overalls, checkered shirts, straw hats. I packed the cupcakes, each with a different farm animal atop the icing . . . a goat, a cow, a sheep, and so on . . . along with the little girls, and we were off, the car full of camp songs and eager young farmhands.

We pulled into the Middleton's long alleé, which led to the stately house perched above the butterfly ponds and the Ashley River beyond. It was an impressive entry as we drove toward the house through the long flat vista dotted by sheep on either side toward the ancient live oaks spreading their mossy arms over several picnic tables. The children were revved up to see the animals as they helped me unload the red-and-white-striped KFC buckets of chicken and squat containers of slaw, mashed potatoes, and gravy. Bacon, the hog, was lying just beyond the fence, a seemingly comatose mound the size of a Volkswagen.

It occurred to me that the food would probably be cold if we went to see the animals right away. We decided to eat first and opened the buckets of chicken and the fixins. I positioned birthday cupcakes on each end of the table.

Suddenly, I heard a noise. One I couldn't make out. The children had stopped talking too and were poised attentively like small hounds listening to the strange thunderous sound. We looked skyward, but the blue above was cloudless. The thundering din was getting louder and louder, and seemed to make the ground tremble. It was a roar now, close and ominous. We turned quickly toward the front gates we had passed through only minutes before, and that's when we saw them. Dozens— nay, hundreds—of sheep, heads lowered, galloping with zeal in their eyes and thundering toward the table in a flying wedge.

They leaped on the benches, they barreled over children, they upended slaw. Striped chicken buckets flew through the air. The sheep snorted and wolfed down chicken legs and snuffled the cupcakes down whole. Straw hats were trampled underfoot. The little girls were crying and wailing, except for the angry birthday girl, who was stamping her foot with a ferocity close to that of the sheep. The awful beasts finally retreated, contented sheep faces festooned with moustaches of mashed potatoes and gravy. I surveyed the sorry sight, hugged the crying children, and cleaned the debris and the little guests as best I could. Nobody said a word on the long ride home.

Historians tell us that Lizzie Borden picked up her ax after being offered mutton for breakfast for the third day in a row. Let's just say I can appreciate that homicidal urge.

I can assure you that there are seven young women and one old broad out there today who can barely look a wool sweater in the eye.

Floored

A class at St. John's Museum is sometimes a commitment and an epiphany. You can pay a fee to take a two-day course in Ukrainian egg painting or advanced calligraphy, but I wanted something resulting in a more substantial creation. So, I chose to take a class in how to make painted floor coverings. The coverings have an authentic American flavor, since early colonists, unable to afford the expensive carpets from England and Europe, painted these decorative canvases and used them on their bare floors. The modern-day floor coverings go for a ransom at design shops, so I figured this was a real economy move since materials were included in the price of the class. The flyer said "two three-hour sessions to complete the project."

What a bargain. Six hours and the class fee to learn something I could use, plus the little-hand painted mat to launch my career as floor-covering painter. Even our thrifty colonist forebears would have taken the hook. I envisioned the Christmas presents all my family and friends would be opening Christmas Day. What I hadn't counted on was the time factor and my own personal X-factor—greed.

On the first day of class, all of us students gathered around a pile of cut canvases that had been prepared with flat white paint. Our instructor showed us how to fold and work the edges into a hem and miter the corners—a difficult task when the material has the flexibility of an unyielding buffalo hide. Next we were to choose our blank floor cloth. That's where I got in trouble. My classmates selected canvases ranging from doily to doormat size. The one on the bottom of the pile covered the whole table. It was by far the biggest canvas.

I'm definitely from the "more is better" school of thought. A satisfying greed washed over me as I wrestled the stiff, four-by-six canvas out of the pile. My ambitious design was to be a fanciful underwater scene of whale, boat, octopus, schools of minnows and eels. Leaping fish, as well as scallops, would border each end in a saw-tooth design. A compass rose was to anchor each corner.

At the end of the first session, I was still sketching my panoramic underwater effort down on my hands and knees. Everyone else was painting. The second Saturday, almost everyone finished the canvas rugs. One teenager put the finishing touches on her Mickey Mouse mat. The bunny mat was finished up and carted away for an Easter gift. I scheduled time in the studio for next Wednesday afternoon. The student with the beribboned goose standing in a puddle, a creation for her daughter's room, showed up for the next two Wednesdays. She and I were the only holdovers from class.

Last Wednesday, with fourteen hours labor already invested, I brought an audiotape of Salman Rushdie reading his collection of stories called *East, West* and my tape recorder. I had fallen under the spell of Rushdie's masterful language, perceptive wit, and intriguing accent, and decided that the beleaguered author of *Satanic Verses* understood confinement all too well and would render the long hours hunched over "THE RUG" less painful. Within five minutes, Rushdie had cleared the room as the goose lady fled upstairs to join the silence of the still-life group.

No matter. I see the next hundred Wednesdays spread out before me while I detail the eyes of an octopus, temper the mournful expression of a whale, and orchestrate schools of minnows and eels through their two-dimensional sea. I've learned a lot. I know why the *Mona Lisa* is unfinished. I understand why Michelangelo's statues, *Captives,* were never completed, never fully freed from their marble by the master. I've also learned some economic facts. At minimum wage and my projected time invested, my floor covering, which I now affectionately refer to as "The Sistine Rug," will be priceless.

The Road to Livingston

Sometimes it is difficult to see where we are if we don't know how we got there. I guess it's like riding in a car and being the passenger. You are talking and listening and because you aren't driving the vehicle, it is sometimes a surprise to realize that you have arrived, at least on the first stop of your destination.

Since we celebrate the birth of Martin Luther King this month, I am reminded of a long past journey, a roots trip I took in 1977 with my thirteen-year-old daughter, Molly, who had never been to Alabama since her babyhood, when my mother still lived in Sumter County. We were going to visit my uncle and cousins, both in and out of the cemetery, and to tend to long-neglected family business. It was also an opportunity to experience a mother-daughter bonding, since the trip to the far side of Alabama took two long, hard days of driving and provided enforced togetherness. The thought of being car-bound with a mercurial thirteen year old was a pretty scary prospect, especially since she could not even do her share of the driving but would most probably do more than her share of the whining. I guess that evened things out. We headed west to the land of my maternal ancestors and my own childhood.

The highway from Montgomery to Selma spread ahead of us on that second day of the trip. I had been giving Molly little mini-travelogues on places we passed or stopped in for a "Co-Cola" break on our hot journey. Atlanta and its environs were part of the scenic tour and running history, which Molly joined in on, since *Gone With the Wind* was a long-time favorite film we had both seen more than once. I dare not even tell you how many times I have sobbed through the departure of Rhett Butler and the death of Melanie, not to mention a few sniffles at the burning of Atlanta.

As we headed down Highway 85, named the Martin Luther King Highway, I tried to fill my daughter in on the events that took place right before the time of her birth: of Rosa Parks' refusal to sit at the back of the bus, the boycott by the black citizens of Montgomery in 1963 led by Dr. King. As I talked on, I realized that I was stumbling along, hesitating, searching for the language to make my thirteen year old understand. It was difficult for my own adult mind to comprehend fully. I picked my words carefully, trying to make her understand the way I remembered the march from Selma to Montgomery in 1964, when the lovely little town of Selma, which I remembered so well from my earliest days, became a word forever linked with a part of the South I tried to deny existed.

We stopped for lunch in Demopolis and as we sat at the table of the Marengo Café, Molly looked at me with eyes squinted in puzzlement.

"Mom. About that Rosa Parks lady. I don't get it. Who cared if she sat in the front of the bus?"

Again I tried to explain how things used to be in the segregated Alabama I remembered and took for granted when I was growing up. How it was just the way things were. Molly shook her head in disbelief.

"Sit in the back of the bus?"

Here, a long pause.

"That's the dumbest thing I ever heard of." Another pause. Finally, "*I* sure wouldn't have done it."

She bent over her cornbread and country-fried steak and started to eat as only a thirteen year old can. I stared at her in wonder and amazement and a feeling I cannot explain to you washed over me—as clean and refreshing as an April breeze off the rolling land of Sumter County.

Fits Like a . . .

Nobody wears gloves much anymore, except actress Diane Keaton, who wears them on all public interviews, including fireside conversations with Baba Wawa—aka Barbara Walters. Gloves are used in winter, of course, but seldom in everyday dressing up, a stage which falls somewhere between wearing sweats and a formal outfit.

Historically, gloves were critical to the social scene. Knights tossed down their gauntlets to expose bare hands, indicating a willingness—nay, a demand—for individual combat. Shakespeare's father was a glove-maker and made a handsome living by making and selling the necessary and ubiquitous fashion item during the Renaissance. Even Romeo wished he were a glove upon the cheek of his Juliet in that balcony scene.

A couple of centuries later, men slapped each other across the cheek with their glove as the ultimate insult leading to a duel to the death. Ladies never emerged from the house unless properly gloved. Think of the key moment in the O.J. Simpson trial, the only critical legal moment in the past century that can be said to have turned on a glove—or, rather, the fit of a glove.

I had a complete trousseau of gloves from high school through college. White cotton and white kid one-button gloves, white kid three- and twelve-button gloves, an assortment of black, grey, beige, brown, and blue gloves for dress-up street wear. I still have the moldy remnants of this ancient collection in a drawer somewhere.

The white kid gloves worn with formals were the most troublesome to maintain. We used baby powder to cover any spots, but it really did not do a very good job. And there was the constant problem of leaving a powdery vapor trail of dust, like the brush of an albino moth's wing, on your dancing partner's shoulder. The other trick for soiled gloves was to make your hands inconspicuous, covering the spotted gloved hand with the unspotted gloved hand, a dicey situation in conversation if you tended to talk with your hands.

I remember throwing my kid one-buttons into the dormitory washing machine at Chapel Hill, and then in the dryer, and being dismayed when they emerged tiny and shrunken, too small for even a munchkin, shrunken like those heads you used to see as souvenirs back in the fifties. (Which makes me wonder, souvenirs of what?)

So gloves have essentially gone the way of the hat, except for special occasions. One of those occasions that required gloves for the very young was dancing school, or cotillion, as they called it in Charleston. Both of my children went dutifully to cotillion twice a month for years, and though I can't guarantee their proficiency in any particular dance, I *can* tell you they learned to speak up in a strong voice, look an adult right in the eye when introduced, and give a nice, firm handshake. That alone was worth the price of the lessons.

My nine-year-old daughter was a reluctant participant at times. She was scarcely at an age to appreciate the rather primitive charms of her colleagues of the opposite sex. She came home one evening particularly exasperated at one young Neanderthal named Charles.

"He's just horrible," she said. "I can't stand dancing with boys. But I did figure something out tonight."

"And what would that be?" I helped her unbutton the white gloves.

"I figured out why we have to wear these gloves to cotillion."

She leaned toward me confidentially. "With the gloves on, we don't have to actually touch the boys."

I remembered that exchange with nostalgia when her teenage years were upon us, and she headed out the door, hanging on the arm of her date with bare hands, looking adoringly up into his face.

Ring-a-Ling?

I had a wonderful lunch this week with Knox, my friend from Mississippi, and her mother Sara and Aunt Martee, both from Mississippi and both "of a certain age." The conversation about cell phones led to an assortment of telephone stories. Aunt Martee said her favorite involved a gruff man who kept calling her number despite the fact that it was clearly an incorrect number. Martee carefully repeated her number, 223-2464, to the man, who slammed the receiver down in her face. The phone rang again. The same exchange took place, the caller getting more irate by the minute. The phone rang again within minutes.

"This is not the number you want," she said sweetly for the third time. She changed her tack. "What number are you calling, sir?" Her voice was cool with Southern civility.

"I'm calling 223-2465," the man said rudely.

"Well, this is not 223-2465," she replied.

"Gol durn it, then," he said, "if it ain't your number, then don't answer the damn phone."

Contemporary phone stories led to the sisters' recollections of growing up in Brooksville, Mississippi, back in the lo-tech days of the crank phone when there was no dial and the caller was dependent on the convivial operator, Miss Addie, to connect you to your party. The operator in a small town was a key player in both social and business communication. Everybody knew her by name.

Miss Addie, on the other hand, knew even more about all of her callers in this small Mississippi town—who was sick, who was having company, who was courting whom, who was ordering goods from Birmingham, who was going to Columbus shopping and subsequently what they bought—everything of any importance within a forty-mile radius. What a power broker in the community.

My friend remembered, staying with her grandmother one afternoon as a five year old, when the elderly lady got very ill. She went to the telephone and told Miss Addie that Mamaw was sick and couldn't talk. Within minutes, Miss Addie had alerted a brother, two daughters, the sheriff, Dr. Hunt, and three bystanders who shared the party line. The grandmother was saved.

Sometimes Miss Addie's help was less heroic but still essential to the townfolk, especially the children. If you didn't know how to spell a word, you just called Miss Addie. She also knew the major river in Colorado and where the Gobi Desert was. She was the schoolchild's best friend.

Miss Addie was not only a literal lifesaver, she also managed to keep the town social calendar straight. When Cousin Sally Beauchamp was having that huge wedding at home with twelve bridesmaids, a telephone call came from New York to the father of the bride. Miss Addie explained to the New York operator that Sally was getting married right that very minute and she couldn't possibly put the call through to the father of the bride at such a time. The caller said that the call was person-to-person and that she *had* to put the call through. Miss Addie informed him that she didn't have to do any such thing and furthermore, the caller best not try to call back until after four o'clock when the wedding reception would be winding down.

Once, a cousin called to say he and his wife and children would be visiting unexpectedly and would arrive by late afternoon. It was already afternoon. Martee called Sara to lament the fact that she didn't have a thing in the house for supper and would be busy getting the guest rooms ready. There was no time to go to the Jitney Jungle for groceries, much less prepare a meal on such short notice. The familiar voice of Miss Addie piped in. "Martee, I have a lovely ham all cooked and ready to eat and a twelve-egg pound cake you are welcome to. Just send somebody by the house to pick it up." Again, Miss Addie to the rescue.

Our ladies' lunch was over. But the vicarious visit to Brookville, Mississippi, during the '20s and '30s and Miss Addie was even better than the fabulous tiramisu we shared with four forks.

Taking Care of Business

That July, my old college roommate, Betsy, and I had already hit Tupelo, Mississippi, birthplace of Elvis, and were finishing up the Faulkner leg of our William Faulkner slash Elvis combination journey. I had even picked up a Faulknerian tick at the fabled Rowan Oak, Faulkner's home, when the two of us got off the beaten path and wandered through Bailey Woods behind the big house. The tick was the Rocky Mountain spotted fever variety, which obviously decided the old broad from North Carolina would make a tasty moveable feast.

"Graceland Too? Oh, just ask anybody in Holly Springs. You won't have a bit of trouble finding it," the girl at the Oxford Tourist Center said. "Graceland Too is open twenty-four hours a day, every day of the year. Fraternity guys are always going up there after a night of tequila shots, at three, four o'clock in the morning, and waking Paul McLeod up for a tour."

Betsy was skeptical. "Just how big is this Holly Springs place?" she asked.

"Not nearly as big as Oxford. Not an intellectual center like Oxford," the tourist center girl said, rolling her eyes meaningfully toward the posters of Faulkner.

Later, tick removed, bite painted with nail polish, we were back in our rental car and off to Memphis, by way of Holly Springs to see the alternative Graceland.

Sure enough, the waitress at the Laurel Springs Dixie Diner gave us directions, adjusted her bra, and did not even look sideways when I said we wanted two "Co-Colas" to go. I was back in the part of the world which does not serve Pepsi and knows how to pronounce "Co-Cola" correctly.

Graceland Too was behind the town square. A seedy white-columned structure, the ersatz Tara's front steps were covered with kelly green Astroturf. Two cement lions, distant and less prosperous cousins of those at the real Graceland, huddled forlornly by the steps, one missing a nose, the other somewhat club footed, most likely victims of those tanked Ole Miss boys.

Paul McLeod met us at the door. We were prepared for an eccentric, but his appearance was startling. Though a man nearing sixty, McLeod was a ghost from the 1950s. His sideburns defied description. His shoe-polish black hair was slicked back into what we used to call a ducktail, or DA haircut, when I was a teenager. His red polyester shirt's plunging neckline exposed more gold chains than any self-respecting Mafioso could boast. The chains garnished his neck and disappeared into a lawn of thick black chest hair. It too looked dyed.

The faux Elvis talked nonstop while signing us up for his perpetual tour. He remarked several times that Betsy reminded him of Priscilla Presley, though it was difficult to discern a Priscilla-like resemblance in this blonde grandmother of five.

The house tour fee is five bucks. Visit three times and you become a lifetime member of the Graceland Too Preservation Society. Many locals were, Paul assured us.

The foyer sets the tone for the tour. Glossy finish 8 × 10 photographs of Elvis, most with curling edges, plaster the walls, coat the stairwell, drip from the ceilings. It creates a shiny, dizzying effect: Elvis with his guitar, Elvis without his guitar, close-ups, profiles, full-length, Elvis with a snarl, Elvis without a snarl. A large sign reads "ELVIS WILL NEVER LEAVE THIS BUILDING."

We were led through a squirrel maze of un-air-conditioned rooms, every surface covered with Elvis artifacts. Several TVs chattered away, monitoring and recording round the clock for any mention of Elvis on worldwide television. Among the oscillating fans, dozens—maybe hundreds—of giant moldy Rubbermaid trunks of memorabilia stood in the dark corners of the claustrophobic rooms, each labeled to indicate its contents.

Paul McLeod, who bills himself as Elvis' #1 fan, droned on in the July heat and even broke into "Heartbreak Hotel" several times, leering at Betsy as he sang. He was sorry we couldn't meet his adult son, Elvis Aaron Presley McLeod, momentarily away on an errand. Paul explained that his wife had left him fifteen years ago saying "it was either her or Elvis." Apparently there was no contest in the matter. The faux Elvis talked on—and on. We found it difficult to extricate ourselves from the tour, since we *were* the tour.

Two hours later, we staggered out into the blinding sunlight, stood dazed and sweating on the Astroturf steps for a few minutes, then lurched for our rental car and the blistering highway to Memphis.

Traffic Court

The citation was for an accident. My fault, according to the policeman, though I must tell you, if that other woman had not had her right turn signal on and had not ended up going straight, well, I would have no commentary.

Court day arrived and I was there an hour early for my 9:00 court appearance, waiting outside the locked courtroom. Soon other miscreants drifted in and we all stood uneasily together until one woman said, "I can't believe I'm here."

No one responded.

"This time I *really* didn't know why I was pulled," she continued.

"What did you do?" (It seemed only polite to inquire.)

"Broke into a funeral procession. I drive one of those GMC trucks, you know, one that has its headlights on all the time? The funeral line eased up and one of the mourners waved me in. I must have looked like a mourner. So I cut in, then cut back out at my street, but a cop saw me and that blue light was flashing before you could say, 'Rest in Peace.' It just don't seem fair." She pulled out a pack of Camels, looked at them wistfully, and returned them to her bag.

"You think that was unfair?" A pony-tailed taxi driver interrupted. "I was caught at a green light and it turned red on me, with me right out in the intersection, and I got nabbed for blocking the street. My passenger even said she would of testified for me, if she didn't have to go back to New Jersey the next day. Problem is, I got three speeding tickets that ain't come to court yet, so I don't know how kindly the D.A. will look on this new case."

The man with the crew cut standing next to me volunteered that he was nabbed for "rolling" a stop sign at the end of his own street, but that he had clearly seen that no one was coming, so his not stopping had not been an unsafe move.

I volunteered nothing. I knew I could not top the lady who had crashed the funeral procession. We were like inmates on murderer's row in San Quentin. None of us was guilty. Simply misunderstood.

We were finally let into the courtroom. Proceedings were late getting started. We offenders, now seated in the courtroom, were all sweating it out as the time ticked by. Deputies from the sheriff's department milled around in the front. A few policemen lingered on the other side of the courtroom. I waited for a suit from the D.A.'s office to show up.

My daughter, a paralegal in her former life, advised me to get a copy of my driving record, pristine for the past fourteen years, and a letter from my insurance company I was to show the D.A. But nobody in a suit appeared. My papers wilted in my hand.

"Hey, no hats in the courtroom. Get that cap off. Show some respect for the court," the deputy barked.

We all jumped.

The pocketbook next to me rang. An older woman reached into the depths of the purse and proceeded to have a conversation despite the fact that the deputy was snapping, "No cell phones here. No cell phones." She finally sent her husband out to continue the phone call.

Suddenly the sheriff's deputies, listening to their walkie-talkies, tore from the gated area in front of the courtroom and bolted out of the courtroom door, hands on their holsters. Obviously an emergency. Bomb threat? Altercation in the judge's chambers? No one explained.

"Must have been a doughnut call," the crew cut next to me wisecracked.

The outcome of all of this? The funeral procession crasher got a reduced sentence contingent upon attendance at defensive driving school, along with the stop sign roller, also assigned to join the driving school attendees. The cab driver got a continuance and is presently drifting through the judicial system with a fistful of citations, like a free-floating astronaut, cut loose from the mother ship. And I? I can tell you, I'll never trust another person's turn signal as long as I live.

The Amazons

As children, we sometimes chose our heroes from comic book characters, fairy tales, the sports scene, or a figure in history, but as adults, our heroes are sometimes thrust upon us. This turned out to be true for me.

Looking around the table today, a stranger would be hard pressed to determine what the common denominator was between these women. Some were of "a certain age" with grown children and were wives of retired husbands. One was single, retired with no children. Another with two preschoolers. Career women, homemakers, tall, short, zaftig, thin. But they were all members of a growing sisterhood in this country. A sorority, if you will, of women united in concern, fear, and hope. They are all survivors of breast cancer.

Their stories are all different, but the intense empathy and connection between the women around the table is almost palpable. They are learning the particulars of the workings of the American Cancer Society volunteer group, Reach for Recovery, comprised of women who have "been there." They have heard the dreaded words, "Yes, it is malignant."

All of these women are survivors, not victims, of breast cancer. They will visit new patients, listen to their stories of discovery of the disease, stories which are all different yet all with unsettling similarities. The women will hold hands with the new patients to cut through the numbness that they too felt years before in the aftermath of surgery and to give each of these novices small handmade pillows to prop under affected arms, rubber balls to exercise traumatized muscles, and booklets to fill in information gaps. Practical tips are passed on. Tips dealing with physical details, specifics on how it really is, generally things only another woman would know and understand.

Each volunteer brings too a walking, talking example of a woman who has shared this devastating event and has emerged on the other side. She can say the word cancer without flinching, without euphemisms, like the big "C," as John Wayne always called the disease. These women can call it by its name. They have met cancer face to face, looked it in the eye, and have not blinked.

As a child, I thought Wonder Woman was by far the most appealing of all the comic book super heroes, mainly because she was the only female in the Super Boys' Club. Like Superman, Batman, and Captain Marvel, she too was transformed from an ordinary citizen (in her case, a secretary) into a patriotic, flag-clad Amazon with a golden lariat that forced all whom it encircled to tell the truth.

Transformation is obviously a key element in the appeal of these characters to children. Their own transformation from childhood to adulthood is just around the corner. The background of Wonder Woman helped explain her metamorphosis. She was part of a tribe of Amazons, women superior in their separateness. Women so committed to their destinies as warriors and huntresses that they are said to have had their right breasts removed in order to accommodate the bow and arrow they used in hunting and in combat, making the drawing back of the arrow on the bowstring more accurate and true.

The heroes of my adult world have also been transformed. But they are not like Wonder Woman of comic book fame, whose transformation was from one persona to another or one of the tribe of metamorphosed and mythological Amazons whose breastless condition was self-inflicted for practical purposes. These real-life survivors of breast cancer have been transformed into grateful women in a much different way, with a heightened zest for living and a more keenly honed awareness of the need to reach out to their sisters—those newly initiated into the club nobody wants to join. These women are true wonder women, strong, resilient, loving, and out to fight the battle of their lives, along with their sister Amazons.

Hats Off

Today I rode behind the Napa Auto Parts pickup truck with its huge blue and gold baseball cap atop the cab. It reminded me that hats are back. The First Lady wears a straw hat while yachting and immediately, less expensive knockoffs are available everywhere. A film star wears the obligatory baseball cap backwards, tiresome symbol of the young, and the accessible style becomes essential to wannabes. But unusual headgear, or at least a twist on the customary hat, turns up occasionally in unexpected places.

Early morning joggers on The Loop at Wrightsville Beach are frequently surprised by one septuagenarian athlete who apparently sees no problem with hairstyling and hat wearing done simultaneously. She wears what I call a "Dealer's Hat," much like those worn by blackjack dealers in Las Vegas. But hers is an appropriate beach version—a pink cotton, open-crowned topper. The difference is that she also wears large pink rollers in the crown of her hair. These pink sausages prove an interesting and arresting sight as she power-walks past other startled walkers.

One of my students sports his unique hat every day. I was somewhat taken aback by this young man sitting toward the left wall on the first day of class. He was sporting a very large purple jester's hat—three points with a purple pompom on each tip. The historical significance was not lost on me, and I waited to see if he were going to remark on it. He didn't. And I didn't. I have long since given up trying the old "hats off inside, please," approach and have resigned myself to the scattering of baseball hats on both males and females in every class. My energy is better focused on MLA format in research papers or the mysticism of William Blake.

The jester student arrived daily, jaunty hat atop his head,

took notes, participated in class discussions, and was totally functional with the jester's cap ever in place. The other students showed no interest in the odd headgear, jaded as they are, and even less interest in the particulars of citation and pagination of the research papers we were working on. I am always amazed at their lack of amazement.

My husband wears a summer hat not frequently seen in these parts, but particularly suitable for our subtropical temperatures. His banana yellow pith helmet is an eye-catcher wherever he goes. Sometimes people even whisper as he passes by. He does look a bit like Bwana Bob, great white hunter in an old Johnny Weismuller movie, but he swears it is the coolest sun-screening hat he owns.

Now, I understand the woman with the curlers. Sunscreen plus beautification does have a very practical aspect. And while my student never explained his jester hat, I assigned a Shake-spearean significance to it, and hope one day he will read and recognize the fool in King Lear. But the pith helmet? Does this mean that my husband's real destination as he saunters out, pith helmet in place on his head, is the swampy marsh? Slogging through the pluff mud? Looking for the elusive wild pith? Or simply another husband—off to mow the centipedegrass lawn out front?

Adding Insult to Injury

I broke my left leg several years ago and, being one who does nothing by halves, managed to break three bones, a spectacular triple break, according to my young orthopedist, Dr. Sutton. Once my leg was set in a full-length day-glo purple cast, I got down to the brass tacks of learning to maneuver in my altered state. Literally feeling no pain on my painkillers, I was shepherded to the therapist to be taught the fine art of crutchwork.

"No, no," the therapist instructed. "To get up those steps, you must place the crutches on the stair and then *swing* your body through."

"But I have on a full-length cast," I said, thumping my bilious purple leg as the proof. I knew I was very close to whining, a singularly unattractive sight in a woman of my years and in my present state.

"You are acting fearful; that won't do," the therapist barked. She resembled the head screw in one of those women's prison movies I had seen on the late show. The tears welled up.

"I *am* fearful," I said. "Only six hours ago I was hurtling down my own hardwood steps with disastrous results. Do you think I'm Errol Flynn?" I muttered. (As soon as the words were out, I realized she was twenty-five years old and hadn't a clue who the swashbuckler was.)

Having flunked Crutches 101, I wound up with a walker that required no expertise. No airborne medal of valor with crossed crutches for me.

My husband began his duties as Nurse Jane with great good humor. I, too, was determined to be the good sport, a role I realize is vastly overrated. He fixed my meals on a lovely bamboo tray and brought them to me in bed. I sipped and supped.

Breakfast with scones, lunch with shrimp salad, and supper with Chinese stir-fry.

By day three, the menu was less exotic. Grits for breakfast, tuna fish sandwich for lunch, and beanie-weenies for supper. Both the menu and my husband's solicitous attitude were going south. At the end of the second week, my Nurse Jane husband had metamorphosed into Bette Davis' Baby Jane without the Maybelline and pancake, and I was the ranting Joan Crawford.

We were very near the grilled parakeet-under-glass episode when my friends began a rotation for taking me out to lunch at various ladies' lunch spots. I now became familiar with heavy restaurant doors Arnold Schwartzenegger would have struggled to open, and one store whose space for the handicapped only permitted opening the passenger door out onto a bark-filled flowerbed where I floundered into crepe myrtle branches, my walker lurching and tilting like a ride at a carnival. I looked much like a drunken sailor released from the Betty Ford Clinic prematurely. (I knew I was in trouble when I began to grade each of the accommodations for handicapped access . . . B- for Talbot's, D+ for the ladies' room at Wendy's.)

My husband and friends were exhibiting eye-rolling and mumbling tendencies that were unsettling. I sensed a hint of mutiny in the air. That old classic film of Richard Widmark shoving the old woman in the wheelchair down those stairs with his hyena laugh flashed in black-and-white in my mind's eye. Except I was the one in the wheelchair.

Six months of physical therapy, countless visits to Dr. Sutton with ever-diminishing casts, and it was over. The summer was mine to enjoy; how I gloried in my newly restored mobility!

On the Fourth of July weekend, our family went to the Fish House for our favorite grilled fish sandwich lunch. Crowded in with vacationers, we waited for an outside table on the deck near the waterway. Standing there chatting with my children, I was suddenly aware of a young man wearing sunglasses edging up next to me. Suddenly, he reached down and slowly lifted the hem of my skirt. It took me a minute to realize that it was my orthopedist in boating clothes, checking his handiwork.

"Looking good," he said.

I resisted the urge to do a small *tour jeté*, right there on the dock.

The Purple Thumb

Gardening for pure pleasure seems to be spreading every year. Americans are becoming almost English in their passion for the hobby. But one friend sighs that she is waiting for what she hopes is merely a fad to literally die out. Her attempts at raising simple houseplants have proven futile and frustrating. She may be the only person on record who has actually killed an air plant.

My husband's gardening approach has always been practical. He usually plants a salad in a small, sunny space in our side yard. Tomatoes, cukes, bell peppers, other salad makings, and at least one experimental vegetable. One year it was a mutation. An unexpected cross between a squash and a cucumber we christened a "squacumber." The interesting veggie was at home in a salad or a casserole. Another year it was okra that produced beautiful plants with star-shaped leaves, which appeared to be flowering and flourishing until an extended heat wave hit in July. The vegetables held up initially but soon languished and sagged in the relentless sun. The okra, in particular, seemed prone to heat exhaustion. The leaves bent back on their stems, prostrate under the blazing sun. A good watering provided temporary relief but soon the droop would return.

My husband's solution proved ingenious, if bizarre. He gathered all the umbrellas in the house, opened them, and propped them over the distressed okra plants. Yellow, green-checked, red print, and one vinyl Mickey Mouse number rose like whimsical flowers over the suffering plants, creating a garden of open, colored parasols. People driving by the house, startled at the sight, stopped to inquire about the unique gardening technique. They all agreed it was a novel approach to a horticultural problem. Unfortunately, the okra succumbed, despite these heroic, life-saving methods. They were taken off the life-support system and were permanently abandoned as an experimental vegetable choice.

My own gardening is limited to caring for a few straggly houseplants which I struggle to maintain in some degree of marginal health. After Christmas someone gave me three lovely glass bulb vases tied with raffia bows, each topped with a large white narcissus bulb. The paperwhites guaranteed gardening success for the gardener with the purple thumb. The bulbs soon sprouted and stretched tall with fat bulbous tips. The latest Martha Stewart garden tip warned against gangly paperwhites. They had a tendency to become heavy, leggy, with a starboard list, a problem which should be nipped in the bud, so to speak. The prevention for this ailment was to administer a shot of gin to the water in the bulb vase. Unfortunately, I lost the article. I had no clue as to the proportion of gin to water. A martini proportion? More on the order of a double gin and tonic? What would produce a vertical buzz for a narcissus? I measured out what I deemed an appropriate belt of Beefeater's for each bulb. Nothing but the best for my babies.

The next morning I checked my paperwhites to see if the buds had opened. I felt as if I had walked in unexpectedly on the aftermath of an orgy. Narrow leaves lolled limply down the sides of the vase. The stems, with partially opened bulbs, sprawled spread-eagled on top of the leaves—wilted, dissipated, drunk after their nocturnal binge on the pricey gin. For three days I tried to resuscitate the bleary bodies. They would not be revived, but lay in their derelict state unresponsive to any hangover cures.

My garden will, from now on, be figurative rather than literal. "I will cultivate my garden . . . " as Voltaire suggested, but in the most metaphorical sense. I should have better luck perusing Marianne Moore's "real toads in an imaginary garden."

Dies Caniculares aka Dog Days

B ecause my mind increasingly segues in mysterious and erratic ways, the last dog days of August always bring to mind earlier dog days in our household, when we received a used dog that arrived with enough emotional baggage to require a porter to get her through the front door. The West Highland Terrier we named Annie, as in Little Orphan, was about sixteen months old. She had grown up without the proper socialization and her behavior was decidedly hostile. We wondered after only a few hours' residency if there were a nearby reform school for terriers, with an opening for the hairy neurotic.

What was this behavior, you ask, that a retired Marine colonel and a schoolteacher could not manage? Annie never came when she was called, which didn't surprise us; when you tried to put her on a leash or persuade her with a gentle hand, you got a snarl that would have done a Doberman Pinscher proud. The black lip curled back over gleaming teeth that seemed disproportionately large for a dog with seven-inch legs. Her teeth snapped repeatedly like castanets in a sort of nervous tic. This dog did nothing she did not want to do.

And the barking. She barked at anyone entering the room, at any noise, at any leaf falling from a distant tree—in other words, all the time. The children took to calling her the HLD . . . horrible little dog.

The dog behavior expert, Barbara Eagles, agreed that Annie was indeed out of control but salvageable. After a private couch session, Annie was enrolled in a beginners' class at DogTrain with five other assorted dogs. A Pomeranian named Spartacus—despite the fact that he more closely resembled Rita Hayworth with his elegant red ruff—was there with his owner, who likewise sported big hair. A huge, uneasy German shepherd named

Felony was the largest student. Daisy, an inordinately shy border collie who tended to lose bladder control when spoken to, a large mixed breed named Darwin, and Bailey, a vocal yellow lab, completed the group.

We all got a black notebook with well-structured lessons and homework. After several lessons, Annie showed some semblance of acceptable behavior. She was definitely not going to be the class valedictorian, not even salutatorian. But then neither was Daisy, whose puddles we circumnavigated every class.

Finally the classes were over. Graduation was to be on Saturday. Guests were invited to attend the ceremony. We invited our son and his wife to come and sit in the family section for the commencement. Refreshments were to be served after the ceremony at a little après-graduation reception.

I was running late that Saturday. I bundled Annie into the passenger seat of the car and we headed off down Wrightsville Avenue. Within minutes I saw flashing blue lights. The police officer was very nice. Did I know that I was ten miles over the speed limit? No, I told him, but I was really sorry. I was going to a graduation, I explained. My dog, Annie, was graduating at ten o'clock and we were running late.

The officer glanced into the front passenger seat at Annie, who remained seated but obligingly curled her lip at him. The officer looked skeptical.

"I have her syllabus right here; she really is graduating." I offered him the big DogTrain loose-leaf binder with the lesson outlines and homework exercises.

The officer began writing in his notebook. By this time Annie had jumped in my lap and was growling at the officer in a manner most unbecoming a graduate of DogTrain.

"Am I getting a ticket? Don't you want to see the training notebook?"

"No, lady," he said. "I've heard a lot of nutty excuses, but nobody could make *this* one up."

Graduation was great. All of the canine students got diplomas rolled with blue ribbon, had a Polaroid taken with the proud parents, and were served doggie ice cream.

But I have to tell you, I *did* unroll the diploma to see if Annie had *really* graduated or had just been given a certificate of attendance before I put it carefully in the DogTrain notebook. Right alongside Officer Jennings' warning ticket from the Wilmington Police Department.

Foreign Languages

As an English teacher, language deficiencies bewilder and intimidate me when I am trying to cope with everyday language dilemmas. I often am convinced that I do not understand the written English language of modern times, that English may not be my first language, though I am at a loss as to what really is my first language. At least I feel that way when confronted with certain written forms.

I recognized the fear early on when Mama made a futile attempt to teach me how to sew. Now, mind you, she herself did not teach me. She did not sew at all, but reckoned that learning to whip up a dirndl skirt or peasant blouse would be mighty handy when I reached those teenage years. A Simplicity Easy-to-Do First Step pattern was chosen by virtue of its having only *two* pieces, rather than by virtue of any fashion dictate. Mama assured me I would soon be ready to tackle a McCall's pattern, considered the ultimate in style by those too young and inexperienced to even think about Vogue patterns. I was hesitant about the sewing but greed spurred my sewing ambitions and I began my project.

It was then that I first recognized my inability to translate the language called *Pattern Instructions*. The tissue paper instructions read: "Turn the wrong side of the fabric to the right side of the selvage edge of the bias of the material." What? I continued. "With the two right sides together, place the wrong side of the bottom edge of the side marked bottom to the top of the . . . " Well, you can understand that this was a shattering blow to my teenage ego.

I still have a recurring language dream in which I have been scooped up by aliens and whisked to a galaxy that closely resembles ours except for the people who resemble those troll dolls and the language. The inhabitants speak a parallel language, but I have not been given the textbook on Conversational Alien, which would enable me to communicate with these strange beings. E.T. call home? I'm trying, I'm trying!

I am allowed only one phone call and one page of the interplanetary phonebook and one minute to complete the task of reaching some source which would hear my plea for help. I page frantically through the Yellow Pages since there is no local alien residential section and, of course, since I faithfully let my fingers do the walking, just as I have for decades now. I know my family is not listed there so I decide to call WHQR, our public radio station. They will have sophisticated electronic devices to tap into the code here and get me back to my own universe . . . but there is no *number* listed! Under the heading of "Broadcasting Stations" there are only cross-references, referrals—See "Radio Stations & Broadcasting Companies"; Also "Television Stations & Broadcasting Companies." Funny, that's what I thought I had looked up. I feel panicky. The alien clock is ticking. I flip quickly to "Radio Broadcasting Stations" as advised by the referral in the Yellow Pages. No numbers. But the new entry reads See "Radio Stations & Broadcasting Companies." I know I am being tested by this parallel language. I am determined to crack the code. Breathing faster now, I rapidly scramble for "Radio Stations, Radio Stations . . . "

Those faithful Yellow Pages mock me. Their indexing system remains an intergalactic mystery, set up to thwart and torture the finite mind of man—and woman and alien. "Broadcast Systems," no, that's not it, "Public Radio," no, maybe "Stations comma Radio" . . . no, no.

I curse those misbegotten, sadistic creatures who have devised the miserable cryptic indexing system of the Yellow Pages and silently place a pox upon their house. My one minute is up. My only hope for human contact—gone forever! Mercifully, I wake up. My dream does make me wonder, though, if written alien may be a lot easier to understand than English.

For Better or Worse

I've been addicted for some time now to reading the Sunday wedding announcements and write-ups in the newspaper despite the fact that both my children are long married. First, *The Wilmington Star-News,* followed by the Raleigh *News & Observer,* a holdover from our living in Raleigh briefly before we moved here.

Until recently, *The News & Observer* put the occupation of the parents of the bride and groom in the wedding article; the *Star-News* never did. I found it a singularly curious inclusion. Usually two sentences at the very end of the article told the reader that Mr. Smith, father of the bride, was a self-employed plumber or a vice-president of Hot Shot Pest Control and that Mrs. Smith was a neurosurgeon or a telemarketer for a psychic network. Mr. Jones, father of the groom, was a professional ventriloquist or tree surgeon and Mrs. Jones was an electrolysis specialist or a midwife.

I never understood what the reader reaction was supposed to be to such a disclosure. Was there some hint of foreseeable happiness or misery of the couple predictable from this occupational information about the parents? I guess it is no more strange than specifics about the educational background and employment status of the bride and groom.

It seems to be part of today's insatiable curiosity and our equally uninhibited need to tell all. We may have carried this premarital snooping a bit too far. Not only do we read about who the couple's grandparents were but what *they* accomplished. Example: "Doctor Smith, great-grandfather of the bride, pioneered the procedure of collagen injection in the lips and was a charter member of the Larchmont Yacht Club."

The wedding write-up may include positions held by the father, such as "President of the First National Bank of Fuquay-Varina"; titles won: "Groomsman: third cousin once removed, bagged the largest impala ever shot on the Serengeti"; honors held: "Grandmother of the groom was runner-up for princess at the ECU homecoming court; father of the bride was a detention hall monitor in eighth grade." Soon it will not only be graduated summa cum laude, but SAT scores of the bride, the bank balance of the groom at the time of marriage, and the fact that the step-brother of the groom is a member of Mensa. Shouldn't we hold back something? Is it a matter of scorekeeping? If so, you should definitely have to give points for degree of difficulty. Just like a diving competition—more points for a back flip than a full gainer?

Previous husbands, wives, children, step-children I *would* like explained. Trying to figure out why all the last names are different, how the hyphenated name works, and the relationships of all these folks is—well, trying. The write-up should clarify these things.

There are facts I do *not* want to know. I like for the article to pretend the couple is not living together at the present time. I don't want to know that the couple returned to Wilmington where they have resided together for the past seven years. I do not want to know the premarital living arrangements nor the sexual status of the couple. It falls under the same category as inquiring why the bride is wearing white although three of her children are serving as flower girls and her teenage son is the parking valet for the wedding reception.

Stand-outs in wedding stories? I *loved* the wedding where the music was provided by the father of the bride—on the musical saw. I *loved* the newspaper wedding snapshot of the artist couple in Chapel Hill who led a parade of well-wishers through the streets, marching from the site of the wedding to a local restaurant. I *loved* the couple whose dog was a bridesmaid in a net ruff matching the other bridesmaids.

With June upon us, I'm gearing up for the new wedding season. With a bit of Lohengrin playing in the background, I can read the newspaper and almost smell the orange blossoms.

A Christmas Memoir in Three Parts

Part II: Turkey Trauma

Fast-forward twenty some odd years from Christmas of my childhood to the holiday house of my married years, when our children were young and my husband's mother and sister joined the family for Christmas. Remember that Norman Rockwell image of that flawless family around the holiday table, faces aglow at the edible symbol of the day, that original "big bird"? Norman most certainly did not spend his holidays at our house.

My less-than-Rockwellian memory consists of quirky holidays with improbable combinations of family customs and personalities. Let's face it. We all think that the way we remember celebrating holidays is the only *right* way to do it. We are all products—or should we say victims—of our upbringing, whether from Alabama, North Carolina, or South Dakota.

One of the major holiday confrontations (and who gets through a family holiday without trauma?) arose each year when my mother-in-law and my husband's sister came to join us for the holidays. We worked our way through the gift openings in the early hours of the day, but eventually the big feast had to be prepared. All went well through the meal itself. We were all in agreement about the essentials: of course, the turkey, sweet potatoes, rice and gravy, Lesueur peas with pearl onions, ambrosia, pecan pie, and the infamous family recipe French Loaf Cake, which I discovered was an alias for the family version of a fruitcake. The elegant change in name did not alter its density, or the fact that you still had nine-tenths of it cowering in a tin the following Arbor Day.

There was a dark family secret which I only learned *after* I married into the clan. It was the après-turkey activity. My in-laws' focus was on the disposition of the carcass of the enormous bird we had just hacked to pieces and gorged on. To me, it was a body to be bagged up, removed from sight, and discarded along with orange peels, pickled peach pits, and wishbones.

But every year the Grahams gathered around the carcass with a single, united goal in mind—turkey soup and turkey hash, to be served on waffles. This ritual, forged through decades of annual reenactment in Wayne County, came as a mystery to the uninitiated like me. The primal culinary ritual was something akin to their worship of the vinegary shredded Scott's barbecue or the consumption of what, to me, was the briny leather of country ham.

The carcass ceremony was unlike anything I had ever witnessed. The group converged on the kitchen, gathered around the island with the forlorn carcass before them. I watched them in a state resembling narcolepsy. Let's face it: I was tuckered out from the fever of getting the just-consumed feast on the table. The children and I would stand back and watch the activity that ensued with glazed eyes. I thought it was important that the little ones see the North Carolina side of the family in action.

My sister-in-law, husband, and mother-in-law crossed and recrossed the kitchen among the pots and pans in a veritable *pas de deux* or (in this case) *pas de trois*. Chopping, shredding, deboning, peeling, and paring, the three moved like a well-coordinated drill team, turning the kitchen into a crescendo of preparation.

I recalled my own family's singular lethargy for days after the holiday meal, and was amazed at this orchestration of sauté pans, stock pots, chopping boards, and peelers pressed into service as the hash was finished and phase two, the turkey carcass soup base, began.

Like sounds from the second movement of a great symphony—more dicing, shredding, and chopping. The turkey bones boiled merrily on the stove. Scraps of meat and bits of onion, carrots, and parsley flew through the air and adhered to the refrigerator and kitchen cabinets. The frenzied finale was the storage of soup and hash into a myriad of plastic dishes that never seemed to have tops that fit.

Finally, it was over. The Graham group collapsed into a satisfied heap, their tribute to long past Christmases completed. A collective memory revisited.

The ritual did *not* include cleanup. The chefs were too exhausted.

One year I snapped. The meal was over. The table cleared. The turkey carcass, surrounded by dirty plates, lay on the kitchen island. My husband and his sister and mother stood gazing at the carcass, exchanging those meaningful looks, well known to me by now. I could feel their old sense of mission and purpose filling my kitchen.

It was only a matter of minutes before the post-dinner festivities would begin. I moved quickly. I got a large plastic bag, darted to the island, and with one deft sweep of my hand, whisked the decimated gobbler remains into the trash bag, twisted an expert knot, marched directly to the outside garbage can, and deposited the body bag of skeletal remains.

No one said a word as I reentered the kitchen. The keepers of the carcass dispersed silently and separately into the living room. We all knew it was the end of an era.

God love 'em. I'd even help with the chopping if they were all back in my kitchen once again this Christmas.

PART THREE

Growing Old Southern

Your Comments Please . . .

I'm often asked, "How do you get to be a commentator? What does it involve?" I can only tell you what happened to me. A friend who worked at WHQR, the public radio station in Wilmington, North Carolina, knew about an opening coming up for a commentator and asked if she could turn in my name as a possibility. Aileen Le Blanc, Director of Cultural Events, called and set up an interview. I dressed in what I considered a hip media outfit and headed down to the Front Street radio station.

Several interesting fellow travelers rode the elevator up with me. I looked at them sideways, wondering if they too were interviewees for the commentator spot or already veterans of radioland. The woman nearest me winked once, then again. I smiled back conspiratorially until I realized she had a facial tic and the wink was to no one in particular.

The elevator stopped at the second floor, where the sign read N.C. Correctional Office Probation Board. Everyone got off but me.

I finally found WHQR and Aileen. We settled in for introductory pleasantries. "Well," she finally asked, "What kind of things do you write?"

It had been years since I had written a short story or essay. I foraged around in my brain for ideas.

"Well, Southern things."

I thought back to an observation I had written a month ago.

"I did a piece a few weeks ago. It was about maimed people." Aileen blanched visibly. I babbled on, hoping to dispel her alarm.

"It's about people who intrigued me as a child. My grandmother lost her right thumb. She had to write with her index finger and her second finger." I talked faster and faster about

Thomas Beale, who lost his right arm. I was struggling to recall which other characters were in the piece. Aileen's face was a mask. The interview was not going well, I gathered.

Mercifully, a knock at the door interrupted my diatribe. It was a friend of Aileen's who had worked at the station some years before—a writer and a deep-sea diver.

"So, how are you?" Aileen asked after introductions.

"Well, not so hot. Had an accident not too long ago."

He held up his hand.

"Lost my ring finger during a dive near a salvage wreck. Caught my wedding band on some wreckage and the finger and the ring . . . gone. "

I was dazed at this existential turn of events. We somehow concluded the interview and I returned the next week with a four-minute commentary on the subject of my choice. It was not about mayhem among limbs and appendages but a piece about the changing South called *Darning Needles and Croaker Sacks*.

The hardest part is the four minutes. I've learned that I'm definitely a five-minute person, but the time slot is very rigid. Editing to the prescribed time is ruthless. I record in a small sound room; I wear a set of headphones. Aileen works in the adjoining room. I can see her through the window but can only hear her through the headset. On the signal, I position my mike and begin. When I flub, I pause and re-read the line. Aileen watches my inflection and clarity. When I've finished reading, Aileen edits my flubs, my repeats, and my curses. She works her electronic keyboard like a virtuoso. I pray that I'm within the time limit.

Ideas for topics? I keep a file box with subjects that look promising. My investment? Several hours to write and revise the commentary. More to record on my tape recorder and to time the length (four minutes maximum). The worst are the hours agonizing on my computer. I hunt and peck, so it is an arduous and tedious task. The trip downtown to the radio station and the actual recording take less than an hour and a half—total.

The miracle of it all is that I made the cut after that bizarre and somewhat off-putting initial interview. I guess they liked me. They really liked me!

Note: Aileen left for Ohio in 1998. George Scheibner now cheerfully suffers through my recording sessions.

Girding the Loins or Gilding the Lions

The end of the semester is fast approaching and I'm almost sorry to see this batch of literature students go. Like refugees from *Pilgrim's Progress,* which they not only have not read but have never heard of, my students and I muddle through the mire of the short story, march briskly around that pond of despair in the frigid landscape of Ibsen's drama, and now embark on the maiden voyage into poetry.

I've developed a unit focusing on poetry and art that involves a trip to St. John's Museum of Art for the visual component (painting and sculpture) and a study of selected verse from our anthology, which includes Wordsworth, Shakespeare, T. S. Eliot, Robert Frost, W. E. B. Du Bois, Mark Strand, and a host of others. The project is engineered to pinpoint themes in the current temporary exhibit at the museum, which can be found in poetic counterparts.

For example: Dangerfield's mythological paintings, "Lotus Land" and "Wood Sprite," recent acquisitions of St. John's, can be viewed as companion pieces to Edgar Allan Poe's lyrical "Annabel Lee" or Margaret Atwood's sly feminist poem, "Siren Song." The students then have to write an essay identifying the themes in each and exploring how painter and poet interpret ideas.

Some students are resistant to the more avant-garde forms of art. One young man from Concord, North Carolina—while viewing an abstract painting—whispered conspiratorially to me,

"Frankly, Mrs. Graham—this is not my cup of tea."

"Great," I whispered back. "I'm glad it's not. Because this is the alternative drink."

Every teacher knows that one of the real perks of this business is humor.

Unintentional student humor. You find lots of it in the answers you get on fill-in-the-blank tests and essay questions.

One memorable essay resulted from our visit to the Barbara Chase-Riboud exhibition of monument drawings, stemming from the artist's background in architecture and sculpture. She developed sketches of monuments to people and ideas that intrigued her. One monument was to Victor Hugo, another to Nelson Mandela, one memorializing The Middle Passage. None of the monuments had actually been built nor would they be. They existed only in the form of the monument drawings.

The students' assignment after viewing the exhibit: to write an essay about a monument *they* would design. The subject of the monument would be a person, idea, group, place, or historical event that was personally significant. They were to explain why they chose their particular subject, the materials used for the proposed monument, the scale of the structure, and a detailed, specific description of the monument's appearance. Except for these guidelines, they were limited only by their imaginations.

Most chose the usual suspects: my dog, family, Mom, my girlfriend. Some moved into the abstract: freedom, love, consumerism. But one essay really captured my attention. This young man wanted to memorialize his fraternity, he said, because it was what had come to be the most meaningful experience of his college life. The monument would be enormous because his admiration for the brothers was huge. The materials for the statue? Solid gold, encrusted with gems. The fellowship with his frat brothers was indeed priceless. The design, he wrote, . . . here he stopped me dead in my tracks.

His design would start with "a base composed of two colossal golden loins."

Yes, it said *loins*. I stopped for a minute to think about it. Yes, that made sense. From what I remembered about that particular fraternity from my own college days, loins were *most* appropriate.

Of course, I knew he meant golden lions—but somehow I liked golden *loins* better. I gave him an A. Because he gave *me* the biggest laugh of the semester.

A Dog for All Seasons

How many of us see our pets as dividing markers to denote the end of one phase in our life and the beginning of another? Our family certainly does.

"That was when Lizzie was a puppy," we'll say, beginning a story. Yet not one of our animals has been of our own choosing. All were *gifts* with the exception of one "found" dog.

The pattern started early. On returning from our honeymoon, we were gifted with a very pregnant cat as a housewarming present. We promptly named the cat ZsaZsa since it was evident that this was no ingénue feline but one who definitely knew her way around.

Our first dog was a found dog, a lovely brown-and-white spaniel-looking beast of unknown ancestry with enormous liquid Saint Bernard eyes. He had been abandoned at the Atlantic Beach motel we had been staying in during a family vacation. Though he had obviously been someone's pet, no one had come to claim him. The motel owner insisted we take him, so we loaded Freebie (as we named him for obvious reasons) into our car and into our lives for the next seven years.

Our next dog, a gift from our son's eighth-grade science teacher, was a black Labrador retriever we named Lizzie Borden, for a distant relative on my husband's side, despite the fact that my mother-in-law was not amused.

For thirteen years, Lizzie was a perfect match for this high-energy time for our growing family. In any family discussion, Lizzie is always remembered as a paragon of canine virtue: intelligent, loving, comical, mellow, and a hunter extraordinaire.

We have suppressed the memory of four telephone cords she happily chewed into fibrous shreds, the half-dozen expensive sneakers she disassembled with her pre-teen teeth, and the food she appropriated without permission and gorged herself with.

Once it was an enormous platter of fried chicken set out on our kitchen island for the Fourth of July picnic. She could snake her neck out in the most extraordinary way. Another time she demolished a pot of hearty homemade chili, cooling on a neighbor's deck. Once she worked her way through a case of chocolate turtles the children had brought home for a fund-raising project, and despite the warning about chocolate and dogs, Lizzie emerged unscathed and mellowed out. Each foil paper had been carefully unwrapped and left untorn on the rug. After each gustatorial orgy, she would return home sated and smiling, her belly tight and distended like an overgrown hairy tick.

Lizzie's long life is inextricably entwined with the childhood of our children. She is in almost every snapshot. Lizzie dressed as Uncle Sam in hat and jacket in the neighborhood bicentennial parade, Lizzie pawing her biscuit treat from her Christmas stocking, Lizzie rolling and "talking" during roughhouse sessions on the floor with the children, a noisy rambunctious activity. Pictures of our teenage children hugging the photographic but greying Lizzie reveal an animal ever patient, ever unflappable, ever amiable.

But that was then. Lizzie has gone to that canine Valhalla. The children have grown up, moved away, married, and gotten pets of their own. After a hiatus of several years, we were again given a "found" dog, this time a West Highland terrier. In our golden years, we have undergone "species shock."

Gone are the languid, laid-back days of Labrador ownership. Our Annie is a terrier . . . or is that terror? This sawed-off shrimp of a dog is wired for action twenty-four hours a day. No more the calm reflective air of our dignified Lizzie. Annie has the aura of a dog possessed.

She is ever inquisitive, always a busybody (nothing gets by her). She is a dog in charge of the world, a very big job for such a small dog. She came to us with a good deal of emotional baggage and is highly unpredictable. Without provocation, she attacks vacuum cleaners, leaf-blowers, chair legs pushed back from the table, empty two-liter plastic Coke bottles, and suitcases.

Undaunted by large dogs in the neighborhood, she stretches herself up to her full twelve inches, daring any dog to "dis" her, as my students say, meaning disrespect. Even Clipper, the over-sized German shepherd across the street, is respectful when Annie is on the scene. Her only competition in the chutzpah category is Maggie, a wild, hyper Jack Russell down the street. Maggie is *so* beyond the pale that she makes Annie seem docile by comparison. We are grateful for Maggie's proximity; she is the "Mississippi" to Annie's "Alabama."

But pint-size Annie is perhaps just right for these years. Our portable grand-dog goes to ride tucked on the shelf in front of the rear window, demands our energy to play a reasonable game of fetch, is patient on a less-than-energetic long fresh air stroll in inclement weather, and requires her fair share of our quiet time. She is a dog for the golden years.

In return for our care, she makes us laugh and gives us her loyal affection. There really is a dog for all seasons.

Iron Magnolia

I no longer regard ironing as a sign of character. As a matter of fact, I never did, despite what the women's magazines tell you. I believe a more significant sign of character is whether or not you refill the ice cube tray after you empty it. Unfortunately, that has almost become an obsolete test with the advent of the icemaker feature on the fridge.

Ironing—clothes that need ironing—I've given them both up. I find I'm buying more and more garments made of flax, a distant cousin of linen, I think, but perhaps in a more primitive state. Flax, like linen, refuses to retain any ironing on a permanent basis. Suddenly, my wardrobe has developed a definite look. My clothes now go with my face for a total fashion statement. In a word—wrinkled. I'm in my sharpei stage of life. It's my golden age of the coordinated look between apparel and appearance, fashion and face.

I even got rid of my old ironing board today. I've had it thirty years or more and it weighed a ton. I must tell you that I felt a bit of regret and nostalgia as I lugged the leaden thing out to the curb for the trash day pickup. The ironing board had layers of fabric and memories around it. The board had survived multiple moves from city to city and state to state, two children raised and now gone on to lives and ironing boards of their own.

This ironing board had witnessed cycles of clothing styles. Those linen sheaths that almost had to be re-ironed midday because they creased faster than you could button your short white gloves. Polyester bellbottoms had endured the super-low iron setting before those *Saturday Night Fever* creations vanished, only to return twenty years later.

The original ironing board cover had long disappeared under layers of sheets which had been safety-pinned to cover the original. Another layer was added about every five years to cover the scorched surface and, of course, the extra padding was good for smooth ironing. I probably spent more time arranging the cover than actually ironing. Each layer became a stratum indicating the passing years, like the remnants of Paleolithic horseshoe crabs and saber-tooth tigers caught at tar pits. It had even been part of the hair-ironing experience my daughter went through when she tried unsuccessfully to modify her curly hair into the fashionable straight locks of the Brady Bunch.

I've had dozens of irons. They seemed to fall victims to various mishaps. I always felt it was something of a death wish on the iron's part. Multiple falls from the ironing boards do cause internal injury, or, just as bad, broken plastic buttons used for the settings so that you have not a clue if you are steaming a fragile silk or spending two hours on denim at a lukewarm temperature. But we only had one ironing board during those decades; the temperamental irons came and went like hussies in a B movie. The ironing board was faithful.

I caught the tail end of Martha Stewart's TV program the other day when she was winding up some helpful tip to bring your ironing to perfection. She went on to talk about how much she enjoyed ironing, especially while watching TV. She advised you to rent the video of *Once Upon a Time in America* and have a whole four hours of uninterrupted ironing. Think of the staggering heap of ironing you could do in *that* millennium. I laughed for almost that same length of time.

Ever the sucker for helpful hints, I used to put damp clothes to be ironed in the refrigerator, as suggested by Heloise. I don't think Heloise ever counted on my timetable and my procrastination where ironing is concerned. I discovered that I have a gift. I can grow refrigerator mold on more than Swiss cheese. So I've now taken to keeping the damp items to be ironed in the freezer.

I always collected ironing until it was worth my while to devote a real effort to the task. I had a box that I kept near the dryer where I put all those waiting blouses and linen napkins. It was very clear as the months rolled by and the box got fuller and fuller that nothing waiting to be ironed was essential to the well-being of my family or the planet. So I would give the clean, unironed clothing away when it had been in the ironing box or freezer for over three years or when we moved—whichever came first. That was my hard and fast rule.

I have to stop now. I want to go stand at the curb and wave goodbye to the garbage truck.

Compu-Speak or "I Don't Do Windows"

Five years ago I received my first computer with Windows 95. It was an uneasy liaison from the start. I had never typed and was vaguely suspicious of all machines, especially this one. The computer sat on my little walnut desk, looming over the back room like the troll in Three Billygoats Gruff. I avoided it for six weeks, hoping someone, perhaps a kindly Billy goat, would remove the menacing thing.

Eventually, when I gathered enough courage to turn the computer on, I discovered my Windows 95 had an attitude. It made rude remarks to me. Remarks you would never endure even from your own children. Signs would appear while I was working on a paper, minding my own business. Signs that said, "You have performed an illegal procedure. If you repeat this error, your computer will shut down." I had no idea what I had done and no intention of repeating the transgression, if I only *knew* what my transgression was. The written tone of voice was one I would not have tolerated from a stranger, much less a PC.

The rudeness persisted. Sometimes the computer would swallow my words, which disappeared as I backspaced, so that I would have to start the sentence over again. Frequently—and inexplicably—my taskbar would droop down onto the printed page as if exhausted, obscuring the paragraph I was typing. Sometimes the page would shrink as if it had fallen down a rabbit hole.

The language of the computer might well have been Swahili. Even the HELP instructions were in this foreign tongue. I would type in my problem and the help column would answer in this alienspeak. It gave me answers to questions I did not ask. It didn't listen to what *I* wanted. Sometimes like a weary husband, it would not respond at all. Like a husband, it had its own agenda and told me not what I *needed* to know but what it *wanted* me to know. I wondered vaguely if my computer had a gender.

I gradually grew accustomed to even fond of, its hostile attitude and abusive tone. Begrudgingly, I began to delight in some of the little devil's parlor tricks. It could count words in a manuscript. It could preserve documents on color-coded disks. It could highlight in day-glo yellow.

In the first two years, I mastered the difference between a file and a folder and how to cut and paste. By my third year, I mastered font, line spacing, underlining, italicizing, and bold. In the fourth year, I graduated to inserting page numbers and moving material from one file to another. I avoided pitfalls: no macros, borders, tables, and shading, which I deemed not only too frivolous, but too complex for my limited computer brain capacity.

To stave off any Y2K disaster, my husband gave me a new computer with Windows 98 and Word 2000 on it for Christmas. The new monitor is huge, as is the new tower and the new printer. The monitor is the size of a Volkswagen. It slurps over the edges of my little walnut desk, leaving no room for the keyboard or printer. The irony of the computer's name is not lost on me: it is a Compaq.

My Windows 98/Word 2000 program has many new features. One is a two-inch paper clip cartoon in the right hand corner, some computer geek's idea of humor. This little sucker has Groucho Marx eyebrows and bulging, expressive eyes suggesting a possible thyroid problem. The anthropomorphic paper clip guy blinks and grimaces. Sometimes he rolls himself up into a bicycle shape and rides into the horizon. He intrudes with important messages such as "A period is the correct end mark for the English sentence."

The little fellow gets so riled up at my incompetence that he contorts himself into a paperclip tangle and rolls his eyes and raises his eyebrows dramatically, just like my children. My blundering has reduced the perky little paper clip to scratching his paperclip head with his loose end wire.

Luckily, I have a whole new millennium to get used to this obnoxious little twit (or to learn how to banish him forever into cyberspace).

Beach Cottage

I teach the use and meaning of irony in my literature class: situational irony, dramatic irony, conversational irony—but I am sometimes knocked out by examples that confront me in my own life. Our family vacation and the beach rental turned out to be a classic example of situational irony. We rented an oceanfront condo and invited our adult children and their spouses to join us at the beach cottage for a week. The term "cottage" turned out to be a case of wishful thinking on my part.

The "cottage" was a three-bedroom condo with oceanfront porch off the living slash dining room. The accommodations were well-appointed and definitely in the glitzy category. All tabletops were glass. All woods were bleached. All floors were covered with wall-to-wall beige carpet. Plastic blinds obliterated all sights of dunes and ocean. Shut the vertical blinds to the balcony and you might easily be in Idaho. The sound of the tide had already been sealed out by sliding glass doors. My attempts to leave the sliding glass door open were successfully thwarted by the absence of a screen door to deter any "see-ums" or "no-see-ums," those miniscule, almost-invisible biting insects which thrive here, so we kept the door closed to the smell and sound of the sea. Sand was not permitted. We were hermetically sealed in our air-conditioned beach condo.

A closer look at the decor revealed a conspicuous absence of actual seashore artifacts. There were no found objects such as sand dollars, pitted conch shells, or artful sea plants—all so wonderful when wet from the tide, but decidedly less spectacular in color when dry. The only decorative touches reflecting locale were the tiles in the fireplace surround, featuring mollusks, nautilus, and various other shells. The tiles were almost obscured by a large arrangement of peach and aqua "permanent" flowers, forever perky in the urnlike vase. The condo had children's videos in lieu of the Candyland games and Parcheesi boards I had wistfully envisioned from summers past. We had brought our own Scrabble and Monopoly and, of course, books to supplement the TV, VCR, and compact disc player. The children quickly discovered the absence of beach chairs and umbrellas, as well as fishing poles and sand buckets. This caused my adult children to regress momentarily into whining about the inadequacies of our rental and the way beach houses used to be at Sullivan's Island when they were children and we lived in Mt. Pleasant, South Carolina.

The parking lot also had signs of a world out of kilter. We noted the many Land Rovers and Jeep Cherokees, shiny and polished. They certainly had never left the asphalt, much less maneuvered over open terrain or even a dusty highway shoulder. They certainly weren't going off-road here. Traffic is forbidden on the beach.

Our trip to Southport, via the ferry, added another ironic observation. As we departed the ferry moorings, dozens of handsome, black-faced laughing gulls ascended from their perches on the pilings and headed after us, hurrying to swoop and careen toward the passengers leaning over the railings of the ferry. These exquisitely marked gulls wheeled toward passengers who offered Cheetos, crackers, and popcorn tossed into the breeze created by the ferry. No diving for fish or searching out burrowing creatures in the tidal pool for these gulls. Not when they could have airborne cheese puffs.

Out of sync? Yes, indeed. Our beach experience caused us to rethink our next vacation and to dream of a beach cottage which really is a cottage. One with wide plank floors gritty with sand, no air-conditioning but lazy ceiling fans pushing the muggy air around instead, and wraparound porches furnished with Pawley's Island hammocks and weathered rockers. We may even get to take a deep breath of that heavy, humid, salt air over the dunes from the ocean beyond and hear the reassuring rush of the tide on the sand.

Eh? What's That?

Usually comic strips bring a smile, or at least a chuckle of recognition, as some cartoonist pokes fun at our foibles. But an old Wizard of Id comic that I keep on my fridge makes me laugh out loud almost every day. The cartoon peasant is reporting a missing person to the constable at the fifth precinct, and the constable is amazed.

He says, "Sir, your wife's been missing a month and you're just reporting it now?"

A long pause before the peasant's response.

"Well," the peasant said, "at first I thought I'd gone deaf."

I'm delighted the cartoonist risked a rap on the knuckles of his drawing hand by Big Brother of the politically correct with this cartoon. Loss of hearing is certainly no joke to those who experience it or to the people around them. But funny situations involving the hard of hearing do crop up from time to time.

Madison Avenue gave a nod to the situation some years ago when they advertised a hearing aid in a commercial showing an older couple in a convertible asking directions. The woman, the passenger, was repeating each direction given by the policeman into the right ear of her husband, the driver. I'm assuming it was her husband. She certainly had the glazed eyes of a woman well versed in the ritual of what I call "translation."

My own husband's hearing has deteriorated significantly in the past decade. We have accelerated past the earliest stages of deafness where I repeated everything the waitress said directly into his ear.

I shout, "She said, 'Hello, I'm Heidi. I'll be your waitperson tonight.'"

Then, "She said, 'The special tonight is blackened Mahi Mahi.'"

And ending with, "She said, 'Ranch, Bleu Cheese, or Balsamic Vinaigrette?'" the salad dressing depending, of course, on the character of the eating establishment. This routine always makes me feel like a guide in a foreign country in which I am fluent in the language of *Waitperson* and translate for my husband who does not speak the language.

Still, no hearing aid. But even he knew it was time for a change after the incident with our Labrador retriever, Lizzie. Lizzie had the unfortunate habit of raiding garbage cans—even in her old age. Since Friday was garbage collection day and all neighbors roll their garbage to the curb, we had to be especially careful that Lizzie was kept in on Friday until after the garbage men had made their pickups.

It was my husband's job to roll the giant green plastic can to the front curb. But he sometimes needed a little prompt both to roll out the can and to make sure the dog was kept in. I usually reminded him early every Friday before I took off for class. One Friday morning, I told him as I was gathering my books and papers, "Don't forget. It's garbage day."

He looked up from his paper. "What?" he said.

"It's garbage day," I repeated.

"What?" He got up and came closer, within a foot of my face, watching my mouth intently.

"It's garbage day," I said slowly and distinctly.

"What?" he asked, looking right at me, very puzzled.

"IT'S GARBAGE DAY!" I was shouting but enunciating carefully. There was a long silence as he frowned back at me, trying to figure it out.

"The dog is gay?" he asked slowly. Again, a pause. "How do you know that?" he puzzled.

Needless to say, we both still laugh at this classic moment of miscommunication. We also made an appointment for a hearing test that very day.

The Loop

Many walkers soon tire of walking The Loop, as it is called. It's the 2.45 mile circle on Harbor Island that crosses Banks Channel twice and takes you down the main drag in Wrightsville Beach. But it certainly suits me, even after five months of almost-daily walking. The measured miles defined by concrete posts with cryptic markings of meters and feet afford a pleasant sense of control and certainty. The Loop is a precise and never-changing circle, the most satisfactory of all geometric shapes.

The daily walk (I dare not give in to puffery and call it a power walk) is a new venture for me and I have taken to careful observation of my fellow walkers and others on The Loop. The age range of walkers is wide, beginning with those in their twenties and stretching well into those hearty septuagenarians and octogenarians.

But attitude is varied and diverse within the age groups. The younger walkers seem to enjoy the exercise the least. Most tend to be a somewhat grim bunch whose intense, set faces seem to be counting some bodily RPM's or concentrating on a vision of endorphin level or abs control. Those in this group, too, are more likely to be wearing a Walkman radio tuning out any early morning birdcalls or the warning moan of the drawbridge siren.

Some of these grim souls are older, however. One sixty-year old-man, a regular on the morning circle, runs with his wonderful set of teeth clenched tightly—as if he were jogging through the fifth circle of Hell. His stoic, pained expression matches his set jaw.

Greetings between passing walkers is another point of interest. Many of the younger group don't bother to speak. They are either too absorbed in their headset, don't know any better, or don't consider older folks worth the effort. No response to my "Good morning." The older people, retirees probably, who don't speak I automatically —and euphemistically—classify as 'Not From This Part of the Country.' I figure they never spoke to strangers at home and certainly don't plan to start at this stage of life. A perverse streak makes me answer my own greeting for them as I pass. "Fine. And how are you?" I answer myself, smiling at my own orneriness.

Clothing is also a part of the changing scene. My son calls The Loop "The Spandex Mile." Those buffed and toned bodies wear halter-tops, spandex shorts, and with baseball caps often in day-glo colors. My age group tends to wear matched outfits— flowered shorts and shirts purchased in Ft. Lauderdale or Boca Raton, or from the Land's End catalogue. As one of my walking friends said, "If you can't get it together at our age, you never will."

Beside the infinite variety of people on The Loop there's an assortment of animal life. Several sets of mallard ducks have early morning snacks around the Presbyterian Church. They glory in the early morning baptism of the automatic sprinkler system. Those more secular ducks hang out around Circles, the ice cream and coffee shop by the bridge, hoping for a bit of doughnut from an early riser. Pigeons lounge on the east side of the roof of the Baptist sanctuary and the mockingbird population is heavy around the cedars bordering the marshes.

My favorites, though, are wild rabbits that live in bushes and hedges near the marshes. Large families of very dark brown rabbits live on both sides of the marsh and are almost always out for sunrise or sunset, grazing in the mowed strip between the sidewalk and marsh, or on the perimeter of the dew-covered soccer field. Big granddaddy rabbits, tiny nervous babies, and preteen rabbits who look you right in the eye, refusing to turn tail and run. You may see as many as fourteen in the morning, or only one. They have become my gauge for evaluating the day as I complete my morning Loop. It's a six-rabbit-day today.

The Fur Person

Animal prints. Leopard spots on silk blouses, zebra stripes on jackets, cougar heads peering from slacks, Cheetah brooches, panther pendants—wild animals of all kinds have become the image de jour in clothing, accessories, and home furnishings. It's a jungle out there.

This is an interesting and perhaps predictable turn of events, since animal rights activists have been so high profile in the past decade. The fashion world has led the pack, so to speak, in the war against the use of fur in fashion. Demonstrations and billboards in conjunction with PETA (People for the Ethical Treatment of Animals) have multiplied in Manhattan. According to *Time* magazine, "Models climbed out of their limos, dropped their white terry-cloth robes in public and as the billboards say, 'turned their backs on fur.'" (Somehow, the image of the male nude models in dead of winter in midtown Manhattan seems less than shocking.) Perhaps I'm getting a bit jaded about the advertising world. It seems very removed from my own world of middle-aged doyennes in New Hanover County.

Maybe it's an age thing. Aretha Franklin recently left her concert in a full-length sable—or was it mink—anyway, something quite outré in this day of raised consciousness. She was heckled and booed by one nearby spectator. The godmother of soul refused to flinch or to respond to the rude remarks and reduced the heckler to "parade rest" with one withering glance. Even a militant from PETA is intimidated by the withering glance of a diva with an attitude.

For those of us with less confidence than Aretha, wearing a fur in this day and age can be a trying experience. Some of us have inherited furs from long ago, when there was no political taint wafting from the pelts. I have a rather woebegone stole which my mother wore in the fifties; I've had it for the past thirty years and have yet to wear it, remembering my mother's admonition that furs and diamonds were unsuitable for young women. The fact is, I am years older now than my mother was when she told me that, but the fur still hangs in the closet—waiting for me to come of age.

My friend Jane was the beneficiary of such an inherited fur—but on a grander scale than a mere stole. She inherited her Aunt Weesie's magnificent stroller-length buff-colored mink. Since Aunt Weesie was well up in her nineties when she passed into the furless great beyond, the animals that sported those pelts in her coat originally shared the planet with Theodore Roosevelt and Lillian Russell. Anyway, Jane took the gorgeous fur to a Raleigh furrier for consignment, knowing full well that she didn't have the stomach for wearing the coat and possibly standing down an angry group bearing gallons of red Dutch Boy high gloss.

Plus, Wrightsville Beach just doesn't lend itself to many days that call for fur. After keeping the coat a full season, the Raleigh furriers regretfully returned the coat, acknowledging that it was unlikely that Jane would ever find a buyer and certainly not one willing to pay anything near the value. The market just isn't there anymore, she was told. Jane and the fur stroller returned to Wrightsville Beach.

These days, Jane never wears the coat out in daylight. Nor does she wear it out socially at night. The coat remains a stroller-length albatross on a coat hanger in the closet, a covert possession. But once in a while, on those dark and frigid nights, when the wind chill is arctic and the moon rises over the black cold waters of Banks Channel, you can spot a lone figure walking a little white Westie and pulling a magnificent buff-colored stroller close around her chin as she takes her dog and Aunt Weesie's coat out for a stroll up and down the docks at Seapath Marina.

Fran and Other Lessons Learned

The lessons taught by a hurricane are legion. We learned them whether we signed up for Conventional Hurricane Wisdom 101 or not. But two revelations that came to me may or may not be on your transcript.

Lesson #1: *Do not evacuate inland to your thirty-something married children's house.* We arrived in Cary just in time for the power to go out. Because of my daughter's age, she assumes that she and her husband are immortal. (This immortality relieves them of responsibility for gathering pedestrian storm necessities such as flashlights, candles, battery-powered radios, or provisions which can be consumed without benefit of microwave or sub-zero freezer capabilities.) This was not the place to be when the wind, power loss, and hurled projectiles began.

Only our cat, Sumter, seemed pleased with the new accommodations. (She must have figured it beat the long-term residency in the cramped Kitty Kaboose which had been home for the past four hours on the trip from Wilmington.)

The morning after the hurricane, a tall pine tree over the driveway promised to slow our departure from Cary to home. But as the sun and the testosterone rose early that morning, four chainsaws converged from neighboring houses, motors revving up to attack the scrawny pine which blocked the drive. In short order, the car was freed up and I left with my daughter mumbling something about her "high maintenance" mother.

Lesson # 2: *Many condemn air-conditioning, blaming it for the demise of community spirit, the death of neighborhood conviviality, and the disappearance of the front porch. But I am rallying on the side of technology and pronouncing AC as the friend of marriage, the purring engine of the world of sleep, and an essential component to civility.* Air-conditioning is the presence and power which permits us to function in the September heat without benefit of animal trainers with whips and chairs to keep us within the bounds and confines of that tight ring of civilization.

My husband, however, is given to nostalgia (or as I call it, revisionist recollection) about his boyhood in Goldsboro, when summer nights meant sleeping on the long screened gallery off the back of the second-story house on Mulberry Street.

The reality is that those long-ago nights must have been as hellish as our recent post-hurricane ones with no air-conditioning, when, exhausted and marginally clean, we thrashed restlessly through the dark hours with everyone else in New Hanover County to awaken as grizzly and ornery as bears cursed with sleep deprivation. Back in Wayne County in the old days, my husband's bad humor had no scientific label and was called "cussedness" or being "ill."

I've always thought, as Dante did, that Hell would be individualized for each of us. None of this "One Hell Fits All" business, but a tailor-made damnation specifically suited to your own transgressions.

My own particular Hell would be that I would be condemned to ride the train between Wilson, North Carolina, and Birmingham, Alabama, with a six-month-old and a two-year-old, neither potty trained, of course, in those pre-Pamper days, none of us sleeping for a single moment of that twenty-six-hour ride, just as I did back in 1965.

The Hell part would be that the train would never reach Birmingham but would barrel through the night forever, never reaching a destination—just me, an infant, a toddler, and a bag of ripe diapers, riding the rails through all eternity.

But in my older and wiser days, I figure this punishment wouldn't be half-bad if the train were air-conditioned. I fully understand the magnitude of those images of burning fire and brimstone now, despite the fact that the Bible never once mentions humidity. That once-feared train ride sure beats an endless night of tossing and turning amid sweaty sheets, waiting forever for a breath of cool air that never comes.

Hurricane Hangover

The adrenaline rush that always accompanies hurricane warnings was definitely there on Sunday. By that afternoon our houseguests had left, the cars were gassed, batteries ready, food and water on hand. Lugging the last outsized terracotta pot of geraniums and the rusty metal dragonfly from the front lawn, we collapsed with fatigue.

Hurricane Dennis was due late tomorrow, according to the storm gurus. About one o'clock Monday morning, it was evident that impatient Dennis was on our doorstep: the wind whistled, we were pelted with driving rain, and lightning illuminated the sky. Then our power failed—always a particularly bad phenomenon for our little dead-end street, since it means no lights or water. We all have wells, and our well pumps run on electricity. All of our water comes from our well: drinking water, sink water, bath water, and, most crucially . . . toilet water. Our inability to flush became alarming as the dark hours ticked by.

We are only a block from the Intercoastal Waterway and have inherited an antiquated electric line that has a history of always —and I do mean *always*—being the last power line in New Hanover County to be repaired. Our neighborhood is part of the city now, although we do not have city water. We've recently been annexed, so we're supposedly better off than we were before. Mind you, we are not in the hinterlands. But, like a wallflower at a dance, our street is always the last to be asked to rejoin the "body electric," to quote Walt Whitman.

Frustrated, I called WHQR, our public radio station, to see if they had a telephone number that might connect me with a human being. My calls to the electric company had all been answered by automatic metallic voices grimly reassuring me that our problem had been "duly noted."

About an hour later, the phone rang. My husband answered it, and when he hung up he told me that a team from National Public Radio was coming over to interview us. We were among the few families in New Hanover County who didn't have electricity, and the media were desperate for material. The hurricane had underwhelmed everybody, and had made for dreary copy. Our powerless world with flushing problems must have been the ultimate non-story.

I threw on some lipstick. (My daughter says this habit is so "fifties," but in lipstick I feel like I'm ready for my close-ups . . . even on the radio.) I also stuck on some red Chinese earrings. Not until I was ushering in the media folk did I realize that I was barefoot. I hoped I looked wonderfully eccentric.

The interviewers were great. They seemed to like my Hurricane Fran story about our eight-day aftermath when we had to go to Hardee's, two blocks away, to brush our teeth, wash our faces, and meet other needs. Even on my best days, I've never been one for the camping life. A week of living out of a public bathroom is difficult for me to classify as an adventure.

I never heard this interview on NPR, but I'm not bitter about not making the cut . . . because today we have electricity, and are flushed with excitement.

Floyd and the Chainsaw Chicken

We knew from the weather reports that Hurricane Floyd was likely to be the real thing, baby. This hurricane we were going to evacuate to Goldsboro, to a local motel. Here's the rationale: it's only ninety miles away, an hour-and-a-half ride. Also, it's my husband's hometown, and though he hasn't lived there in forty years, it promised that reassuring cushion of familiarity.

Arriving too early for check-in, my husband and I drove around. He pointed out the landmarks: "There's the old Goldsboro High School. Did you know that Andy Griffith used to teach drama there? And there's where Cuttin' India's house was, next to Mawmaw's. Did you know that . . . "

Suddenly, hurricane nerves kicked in. Did I *know*? Did *I* know? I was not exactly his date. I have been married to this man for more than thirty-eight years and even lived in Goldsboro for fourteen months myself when he was in Vietnam. We drove on without the nostalgic litany.

That night, ensconced in our motel, we heard the rain and wind howl. We were starving from our frenzied evacuation, and were glad there was a restaurant in the building so we didn't have to brave the weather. Called the Crossroads Country Café, the restaurant featured an extensive buffet of country delectables, according to the sign in the lobby—and for only $4.25 including beverage!

As we entered the doorway of the dining room, an enormous eight-foot-tall creature loomed over us. It was an amazing sight: a giant chicken——a rooster, to be exact. The animal was white, with a red comb and chrome-yellow beak and feet. The scale of the wooden sculpture was impressive.

On closer inspection, I recognized the features of the bird. It was Foghorn Leghorn, the character from the cartoons of yesteryear. You remember, the one with the distinctive Southern accent: "A real Southerner, boy . . . Deep South, that is."

The hostess told me that the artist was a local who lived out on Highway 117 and had carved the remarkable bird with a chainsaw from a single log, except for the three tail feathers, which had been carved separately and inserted at a jaunty angle.

"Is it the Leghorn chicken character from the cartoons?" I asked.

"Well, yeah, but"—she leaned in confidentially—"we all call him Earl."

The sculpture was an *objet d'art* with a practical purpose. Tucked under one wing, a chalked message on school slate read, "Hey. Come on in and have a seat." So we did.

The buffet was as remarkable as the giant chicken. Hot biscuits, cornbread, tiny field peas and snaps, white corn cut from the cob, string beans, squash, sliced tomatoes and cukes, huge trays of red jello with all sorts of fruit cut up in it, and the requisite Southern dessert, homemade banana pudding.

The meat was another thing: fried chicken, cut by someone with no knowledge of the bird's anatomy. Even Earl would have had problems recognizing a cousin. Then came the pork offerings. I had difficulty identifying most: chitlins, lean strips pulled from the ham hock, hog jowls, and large chunks of "the other white meat" with what looked like lard on them. I decided to go vegetarian.

We were sad to leave Earl, the magnificent giant chicken, after our breakfast the next morning. Our evacuation destination had been a successful choice: we never lost power, the food was hot and plentiful, and Earl's hurricane hospitality was hard to beat. He never lost the smile on his beak.

Now, getting home was another story.

Grandmère

Motherhood and grandmotherhood are rites of passage very much on my mind since I'm scheduled to embark on my new status this summer. Granny Yokum and Grandma Moses are images I'm trying to suppress.

I am preoccupied these days with all babies. I watch commercials with babies in them with heightened interest. I crane my neck to inspect infants in strollers and inquire about the ages of total strangers' babies, trying to refresh my memory about the look of a three-month-old versus the expression of an eight-month-old, nuances that have faded from my memory.

I've always heard you were getting old when your own baby reached thirty years old, but no one warned me about the realities of becoming a grandparent. Reaching the new status is almost as traumatic (and *conflicted* as they say) as being eligible for the senior citizen's coffee at McDonald's. But I'm accepting the bid of that sorority out there that used to be composed of blue-haired old ladies. Not today. Now they go blonde and undergo extensive cosmetic surgery. I'm joining the new corps of swinging grannies—Naomi Judd, Elizabeth Taylor, and Lauren Bacall.

There are so many profound aspects of this new role: a fresh life in this jaded world, someone who will toddle through the 21st century, the new millennium, with all of its hopes and fears. Heady stuff, this.

But names are first on the agenda. Names. Naming the baby? No. Not my job. The question is—what will *I* be called? *Grandmother* seems entirely too dignified, since I have elaborate plans to be a perfect fool about this baby. *Grandmère* is entirely too outré, even for my taste. Besides, I could never pull it off.

Mamáy—that's what my husband and his siblings called my

dear mother-in-law; *Meéma*—too reminiscent of a braying donkey; *Mimi*—too Follies Bergère; *Mamaw, Granny* (God forbid!)—too Flannery O'Connor.

I remember that moving scene in the old film *Anastasia*, the one with Ingrid Bergman as the wannabe Romanov grand duchess and Yul Brynner as her mentor. In one scene, Ingrid tries to convince her grandmother, alias Helen Hayes, that she, Ingrid, is the real lost Anastasia. The grandma, last of the ill-fated family of the tsars, recognizes Ingrid's telltale cough as authentic—a nervous habit of the child, Anastasia. Ingrid embraces Helen. "My-yen-kié-ya" (or something like that) Ingrid whispers gratefully and they weep in a surge of violins and pained expressions. It's a very moving moment. And don't you love the sound of the name: My-yen-kié-ya? Or did Helen Hayes whisper it to Ingrid? Of course, I don't really know that the name means grandmother at all, but if it doesn't, it should.

Pretentious? You bet! I've considered this as a unique and appropriately grand title, but have decided that I'm really not up to it. I'm not the Helen Hayes type. And what if it doesn't mean grandmother? What if it means "You Old Fraud" and Helen is saying it to Ingrid? I don't have any Russian resources to bounce this off, so I believe I'll pass. And now that I think of it, doesn't "babushka" mean grandmother? Forget that. It's not even in the running.

Derivations of my own name are possibilities, though anyone who *ever* called me Nanny in my presence has done so in peril of severe pain and possible mutilation. I'm leaning in the direction of "Nana" as a possibility. The Nanas out there are of dubious literary origin. There is Nana, the enormous dog in Sir James Barrie's *Peter Pan*, who is nursemaid to Wendy and the Darling children. Then, of course, there's the novel *Nana* by Emile Zola, which caused a Parisian scandal in the 1880s because his heroine, Nana, was a prostitute. (My, how our literary perceptions have changed.)

Nana. I like that. Just the right literary blend of Barrie's canine devotion and Zola's risqué business. The baby can call me Nana. Or anything else. Just as long as she calls me.

Caroline Time

Mark Twain said: "There are two ways to travel: first class or with children." Our recent experience with our first grandbaby taught my husband and me new aspects of time, travel, and food when an infant is involved.

This past week, we had our nine-month-old granddaughter, Caroline, here with us for five days. So what, you say? We all have the grandchildren come for a visit. But this visit was unique because the parents were not here. Just Nana, Grumpa, and baby Caroline.

In a fit of unbridled optimism, Grumpa Ernie bought a colorful playpen named "The Happy Camper" (which he hoped was an omen for a self-fulfilling prophecy) and a high chair; we borrowed a portacrib. We were ready for the great adventure.

Caroline arrived in a caravan of accessories and accouterments, luggage and equipment. A mind-boggling array of *stuff*—stroller, Baby Björn front-carry backpack (requiring a minimum IQ of 186 to attach to your body and render functional), a swing to hang from the door jam, an exersaucer (a sort of extra-terrestrial looking bouncie seat which whirls around like the Tilt-a-Whirl at a carnival), and a baby monitor with two-unit communication (a mechanical umbilical cord between the baby and you). Her extensive trousseau would make Madonna's baby Lourdes pea green with envy. Cool weather outfits and resort wear were unpacked since the weather is so unpredictable right now. Bottles, formula, baby foods, bibs, burping cloths, crackers, Cheerios, and enough pacifiers to plug every infant mouth in the county were disgorged from the luggage. A cosmetic bag stuffed with enough items to satisfy any diva—Desitin, baby wipes, Pampers, soapless shampoo and body wash, Motrin for teething, sunscreen, tiny sunglasses, emergency ipecac for inducing vomiting. This list does not start to cover the toys.

Working all this equipment is another thing. You think childproof aspirin bottles are tough. The baby accessories seem to all be senior-proof. Catches, locks, fasteners, brakes, latches on car seats, high chairs, strollers, swings, bouncie seats, and happy campers made me long for those unsafe, insensitive days when we plopped infants in a car seat hooked over the front seat and the toddlers rattled in the auto interior like loose beans in a jar.

My son swears to this day he has brain damage when, as a four-year-old, he rode (unstrapped) in the front seat of the car with his seventy-year-old Mamay in Goldsboro. When she slammed on brakes for the *other* persons' stop signs (as was her custom), his head would bounce against the dashboard like the ball on a bolo-bat.

I discovered that five days is a very long time. Maybe time with babies is like dog time, where one year of human time equals seven canine years. Time, which used to be measured and orderly, becomes elastic or compressed with an infant. When you think of a five-day vacation, it doesn't seem like any time at all. But five days with a nine-month-old? Try to grasp the idea of the endless reaches of space.

Meals were interesting. Caroline has her own timetable for this activity, since she likes to feed herself but cannot manage a spoon and has no teeth to speak of. She handles all finger foods with the care and speed of a technician handling radioactive waste. During lengthy pauses, you try to spoon some food in her mouth while she is concentrating on the radioactive transfer. Squeezing any uneaten vegetables between her fingers and onto her head signals the end of the meal.

One night, Grumpa Ernie brought in cafeteria food: turkey, dressing, sweet potato soufflé, and snap beans with enough sodium to meet an adult's daily minimum allotment in each bean. Three days later, I was still finding sweet potatoes behind Caroline's ears and in her eyelashes.

Caroline's accomplishments at nine months: she can sleep from eight PM to seven AM, wave bye-bye, drink out of a straw, blow you a kiss, find her pacifier and plug herself with no help at all, and smile a smile that would melt the heart of Saddam Hussein.

I had fifty-five minutes to work on this commentary—the length of Caroline's morning nap. Talk about time telescoping. I hear her waking up now. She is going home tomorrow. I miss her already.

The Heart of the Matter
(A Funny Thing Happened to Me on My Way to the Bypass)

In the pitch black we headed out to the hospital for our 4:45 AM check-in for the bypass surgery. My husband, Ernie, was to be rolled to the operating room by seven AM. My son and his wife, Debbie, met us in the holding room. We all joked and made nervous wisecracks to ease the waiting. An enormous, formidable woman named Lou-dean came in to give us the flight plan. First, taking an antibacterial shower. Next, donning hospital garb. Then shaving the body from head to toe. Last, the morphine drip. Lou-dean gave Ernie the antibacterial soap and said ominously, "I'll be back for the shaving," her voice faintly reminiscent of someone on intimate terms with Morticia and Lurch. I thought Ernie flinched, but maybe not.

We stepped out while Lou-dean entered, razor in hand. Ernie was very animated, unseemly for such an early hour. I recognized the babble of sheer terror.

Blessedly, the morphine drip came right on the heels of Lou-dean's departure.

The morphine had taken the edge off for Ernie. Actually, more than the edge. He was drunk as a lord.

"Do you think I could get some more of this stuff?" He blinked his eyes in slow motion and grinned a wide, dazed smile.

I mumbled something about being sure he could, but it had been a rhetorical question. He was already holding forth on a new topic.

It was well past seven now and still no move toward going to the operating room. No word about the delay came from the personnel. It was of no consequence to the patient. Ernie was happily singing some bawdy song he had learned in the Marine Corps. I hoped the floor nurse wasn't within earshot.

About eight o'clock my son went on to work; we were to keep him posted by cell phone. Another hour dragged by. I was uneasy; something must be wrong. Ernie was oblivious. He lectured Debbie about being chased by a grizzly bear fifty years ago in Alaska, an oft-repeated story of his. His arms flailed wildly. Debbie's glazed look was similar to Ernie's, but without benefit of morphine.

Eventually, the nurse came in and explained that the air-conditioning had been shut off to our assigned operating room, whose walls were now sweating like a rain forest in the June heat. The bypass operation was rescheduled for the next day. Ernie was deep into his Alaskan story.

"I guess we will have to get him upstairs to his hospital room and regroup tomorrow," I said.

"Oh, no," the nurse said, "he will have to go home and come back again at five AM tomorrow morning."

I looked at my husband who was finally asleep now, snoring softly.

"Take him home? Like this? He can't even open his eyes, much less focus."

Somehow, we poured him into the car and headed through the morning traffic toward the beach, Ernie's seat belt securely strapped since he was too limp to hold himself upright. He opened one eye and looked benignly at me.

"You'll have to open both eyes," I said. "You look like a pirate —or a lech." He nodded agreeably, continuing to look at me with the one eye. It was getting on toward 11:30.

"I'm starving," I said to Debbie as we drove out Shipyard Boulevard. "How about we stop off at the Salt Works? Best grits in town."

"How can we manage it with him? He's as limp as a dishrag." She nodded her head toward Ernie, who had momentarily dozed off, listing slightly to starboard, held fast by the sling of his seatbelt.

"With one of us on each side, we can walk him in. Just like

the movie *Weekend with Bernie* when they took the dead man to the cocktail party," I said. "You want to do that, Ernie?" I nudged him gently.

Ernie's eyes rolled up into his upper lids, his head flopped to the left, and he gave us a long, confused look before closing his eyes. We took this as a "yes," put on his hat, and headed for the restaurant.

We put his sunglasses and hat on as we exited the car. Somehow we managed to get him inside the tiny restaurant to the wooden booth and to slide him in so that I would be outboard. I positioned him like a display rag doll in the corner of the booth. The sunglasses fell off, but his hat remained at a rakish angle and we decided he was less conspicuous with it on than off—his eyes were less noticeable and besides, this was a hat-wearing kind of eatery.

The waitress took our order and tried not to stare at Ernie, who had returned to his roué look (one eye closed, the other unblinkingly open) and kept nodding his head agreeably at everything she said. We ordered a bowl of grits and some toast for him—it seemed a bland, hospital-like choice for an ex-patient. We had no clue if he could actually eat it.

Breakfast did not go well. Ernie was slumping badly by the time the food arrived. Both eyes were closed now and he was making a rhythmic, gentle whistling sound which threatened to grow louder. His head nodded perilously close to his uneaten bowl of grits and I tried to recall the name of the old movie where the man fell forward while seated at the dinner table and drowned in a bowl of soup. I moved the grits away from the target zone in front of him.

Getting a doped man into a car is tough, even with two of us, but eventually we stretched him on the back seat, drove home, and unloaded him into a bed—to sleep round-the-clock and awaken the next day for a repeat of the predawn ride.

P.S. The heart surgery the next day was a complete success. Ernie doesn't remember anything that happened the day before but has given permission for the telling of this story.

Like a Virgin

(Luddites of the World, Unite!)

Luddite is a term you see from time to time in articles on the exploding info-glut of the Internet and the information highway, or in articles analyzing Ted Kaczynski, the alleged Unabomber. Ted represents the far end of the Luddite spectrum. Luddites, those British workers who, between 1811 and 1812, rioted in the factories in England, protested the use of large textile machinery, believing that the Industrial Revolution and the new-fangled machinery would mean the end of the working man and life as they knew it. They were right, of course.

They stormed English textile factories and smashed the knitting machines and mechanical looms. This protest was taken rather seriously by the British, who quashed the movement by hanging the perpetrators by old-fashioned rope and gallows. So, the term Luddite has come to mean anyone opposed to the advance of technology because of its dehumanizing effects on society and the individual. This concern has been the time-honored focus of philosophers, poets, and economists for the past century. The pros and cons of England's industrial revolution were as hotly debated in the nineteenth century as technological advances and their accompanying ethical problems are today.

This is not a weighty tome on our evolving world but rather a tiny observation on a personal level. You see, I'm a closet Luddite, a neo-Luddite. There, I've said it and I'm glad! I too have rages when the Xerox machine refuses to spit out a copy and lights up strange icons indecipherable to me. I do my best to remain cool (the premier state of mind, according to my students).

I repeat the steps that have always produced the desired results in the past, but because of the way I'm holding my mouth, or the proximity of Saturn to Uranus at this particular moment, today the Xerox machine refuses to perform and simply lights up another cryptic icon which flashes at me accusingly. I try to remain calm, despite the fact that I have class in four minutes and need this copy now. The ultimate humiliation is when I have to report to the office manager that I have failed at the Xerox machine and cannot produce a duplicate without help from a more left-brained being.

I'm one of those creatures who does not type, a definite handicap to a person who was an English major and has spent virtually her whole life teaching, making out syllabi, schedules, and lesson plans. Well, you get my drift. This omission in my education has been costly in time and money. Time to find, deliver, and pick up all my written work, and the typing fee to boot. At this late date, it may seem strange that I would invest in a computer, since on most fronts I have been known to be dragged kicking and screaming into this age of technology, incivility, and bad grammar, but I finally gave in to the pressure.

This commentary was written on my computer and I will tell you that it has only taken me the better part of the day to whip this out. So much for time saving. Now for money. Well, let's just say that this is a very pricey typewriter. My one big advantage is that I have no bad habits to eradicate and nothing to unlearn. I am a true *tabula rasa*, so to speak.

When I went to the University of North Carolina-Wilmington library today to look up some details on the Luddites, I found an entry in the on-line catalogue. As I moved to the printer for my printout of the entry, the room suddenly darkened, the whirr of the computers stopped, and we were plunged into that velvety dark silence we all recognize as a power failure. It struck me, there in the dimness, as a powerful coincidence— that cessation of every mechanical instrument in this cavernous repository of books and documents at the very moment I was researching Luddites. I felt a sudden surge of power myself. As I stumbled out of the darkened library, I wondered if perhaps there is a local chapter of the Luddites—looking for converts.

Luddite in Training

I knew I would get this Christmas gift because it is electronic. If it has an electrical plug on it, my husband Ernie will buy it. It must be a male mind set: if it plugs into an electrical outlet, it is a good thing. I've often wondered why some smart marketer doesn't put a plug on a sofa or wing chair or hutch to cater to this male market. Furniture would fly out of the store.

Anyway, I wanted a cell phone. It seemed like a good idea for trips. What if the car should break down? What if I'm running late in a thunderstorm and can't make it to a pay phone, or if I don't have thirty-five cents? For emergencies only, of course. Only in the most urgent and extreme situations would I actually *use* the thing. I would not join the rude ranks of those for whom the bumper sticker "Hang up and Drive" was designed. I *would* not talk on the phone over my open-face pita salad at lunch in a restaurant. I *would* not have my evening bag ring during the ceremony while the mother of the bride was being seated on the left side of the church. I *could* not walk down Market Street toward the river carrying on an animated conversation, mindlessly jostling against passersby.

Anyway, here we are eight weeks after Christmas and I'm *still* trying to master the operation of my cell phone. I have to tell you that old saw about "being careful what you wish for" is gospel. After all, this phone is a technological device. It has many symbols on it. Tiny red and green receiver icons, open book icons, plus and minus signs, stars, a sign that looks like Mickey Mouse ears, icons that look like the printed symbols writers use for cuss words. I come from a long line of people with no discernible left-brain function. My only real mechanical accomplishments are that I can program a VCR and drive a car.

The younger generation cannot fathom this mechanical ineptitude on the part of us seniors. My son has made numerous trips to the house since the holidays on cell phone training missions. He has patiently gone through the instructions, talking slowly as if speaking to a very small or very backward child. I noted that on the seventh instructional round on reading the recharge battery icon, he had begun mumbling in exasperation that politically incorrect phrase, "You people . . . " This is a tip to seniors that the generational gap is always with us.

Learning the cell phone is a big job. I must even remember to recharge my battery, a difficult assignment for someone who can't remember to take a multivitamin once a day.

My husband, a fan of espionage movies, now uses the phone as a tracking device, similar to those surreptitiously attached under the car bumper of the unsuspecting hero by some villainous agent. The initial emergency use of the cell phone we envisioned has been superseded by this new application. The fact that I have unlimited free incoming calls but must pay for outgoing calls gives rise to Ernie's new policy: "Don't call me, I'll call you."

My retired husband can now track me down anywhere. Amazing, when for thirty-eight years he had only a vague idea where I was 90 percent of the time and it didn't bother him a whit. It's a remarkable turn of events. My cell phone now rings in the depths of my pocketbook in the ladies' room of the Phoenix Café, it rings persistently from the bookbag in the back seat of the car, it rings under my pile of clothes in the dressing room at T.J. Maxx. My purse rings in the middle of a class lecture on the differences between onomatopoeia and oxymoron and on the poetic principles of Edgar Allan Poe.

I have begun to think of myself as a female Jean Valjean in *Les Miserables*, hounded by the relentless pursuit of Inspector Javert, aka Ernie. If only I can master that "power off" button.

Bridge Over Troubled Waters
or The View from the Bridge

I have had a profound fear of bridges since I was a child. In the 1940s a portion of the Cooper River Bridge, which spans the Cooper River and joins Charleston, South Carolina, to Mount Pleasant, fell into the river late one Saturday evening after a freighter broke loose in the night and damaged the supports. Unbeknownst to the Sunday drivers, part of the bridge had collapsed in the middle, leaving a great abyss. Several cars, families inside, drove onto the bridge and plummeted into the water and were lost. The headlines and photos in the newspaper were frightening and memorable. I had dreams about that story as a child.

I carried these terrors of falling bridges and collapsing spans into adulthood.

While living in Manhattan, going to the boroughs or anywhere out of the city in a car, I crouched low in my seat, head down, and refused to look out of the window. I was not a cute date on those occasions.

Years later, we lived in Mount Pleasant while the children were growing up and I will have to tell you that white-knuckle driving over the Cooper River Bridge never left me.

The family arrived in Mount Pleasant on our way to The Citadel in Charleston after a long trip from Camp Lejeune, North Carolina. We were traveling in two cars. I was in the Nova wagon with Molly, age six, and our cat, who for some reason had been hanging from the cloth ceiling of the car like a bat for the past eighty-six miles. Ernie was in the other car with the dog and our eight-year-old son, Howell. As we approached the bridge at dusk, I signaled Ernie to pull over.

"I don't think I can do it. I can't drive over that bridge."

"Of course you can. Just grit your teeth and do it." My husband—ever the Marine.

We entered Charleston, the cat still hanging from the cloth ceiling of the car, Molly huddled on the floor, and me, sweating profusely in the January cold, muttering through clenched teeth, "I can do this, I can do this." It was a less than auspicious entry.

But this same terrifying bridge was the setting for a funny bridge story. Jeanne, a friend of mine, and her husband Will had bought a new mattress in Charleston and the salesman had lashed it firmly to the top of the car for the trip back to Mount Pleasant. The queen-size piece, sealed in heavy plastic wrap, was secure, but the plastic ends made an aggravating flapping sound in the wind as they headed onto the Cooper River Bridge and up into the tallest part of the span. Just as they crested the span, they heard a swooshing sound and Jeanne looked back to see the new mattress hit, bounce, and slide to a stop on the bridge roadway behind them, barely missing the car following them. Jeanne told Will they had to stop immediately and retrieve the mattress. She had waited two years for a new bed and she was not about to abandon it in the middle of the bridge. Will took one look at the traffic and kept going.

When they got to the Mount Pleasant side, they turned around and headed back over the bridge to recross and retrieve the ill-fated bedding. They reached the upper span. No mattress. It was gone. They were stunned. What could have happened to it? It had only taken a few minutes to turn around and come back to the spot where the mattress had sailed off. It was a puzzlement.

Disheartened and bewildered, they turned around again and headed home to Mount Pleasant. As they rode on down the highway they saw an ancient station wagon slowly making its way in the right lane. It was creeping along at fifteen miles an hour and as Jeanne and Will approached they saw six hands stretched upward, holding a plastic-wrapped mattress carefully atop the wagon. The arms looked like human grappling hooks attaching the mattress to the roof of the station wagon.

Jeanne was outraged. "They've stolen our mattress," she shrieked.

Will flagged them over. "You guys have a mighty fine mattress there," he said in a mild voice to the driver.

"Yeah. It's brand new too," smiled the driver proudly. The other inhabitants of the car nodded and grinned in agreement.

"I sure could use a mattress like that. How about selling it to me? Will twenty dollars do it?"

The deal was done and Will helped the mattress entrepreneurs transfer the mattress to the top of Will's car and lash it down with the ropes that were still atop his car.

"I'm much obliged," Will said in his courtly low-country way.

Jeanne was livid. "You paid them for our own mattress!" She was fuming.

Will nodded, smiling serenely. "It was worth a lot more than twenty bucks not to have to take my life in my hands to rescue the damn thing from the bridge," he said, turning the station wagon onto their street. They listened once again to the plastic covering the mattress flapping in the wind as they headed for their house.

There's a Word for It

It's been around a long time—this idea that the only thing you can really count on is change. Around 510 B.C. Heraclitus said:

> *All is Flux, nothing stays the same.*
> *Nothing endures but change.*

Over 2000 years later, Honorat de Bueil, the Marquis de Racan, restated the Greek epigram in French, as the French are wont to do, and declared:

> *Nothing in the world lasts*
> *Save eternal change.*

Nowhere is change more evident than in the mutation of language. It is the nature of this fluid element to morph itself into other forms or generate new words and idioms. Take that word *morph*. Were you using it fifteen years ago? Not only was I not using it, I didn't have a clue what it meant.

Buzz words come and some go. That's the nature of the beast. But occasionally word changes really aggravate me, a sure sign of advancing age and latent curmudgeonliness.

Take *B.C.*, since we were quoting old Greeks. How offensive can that term be? Do we have to use *B.C.E.* these days: *Before the Common Era*. Do we really want to be part of what is called the common era? *Common* is a word I was not even allowed to use growing up in Alabama. Mama insisted that we never say that anyone was *common*. If we had to voice that particular opinion, we were to say they were *ordinary*, which, in her vocabulary and tone, said it all. I will continue down my politically incorrect path, since I find it next to impossible to remember that *B.C.* is now *B.C.E.*

And when did those few exotic countries you remembered from grade school geography, which conjured images of a jungle fantasy, get replaced with less fanciful names? I miss the mystery in the name Burma, officially Myanmar since 1989. Myanmar—sounds like a new plastic product that hermetically seals your toothbrush. "New design, now sealed in Myanmar—for your family's safety and protection." Now what was wrong with Burma?

Who would vote for Sri Lanka, which sounds as if it were invented by a committee, instead of the melodious Ceylon? And Thailand in place of Siam? Anna and the King of Thailand? I think not. And I do miss the drumlike resonance of the Belgium Congo.

The newspapers are partially responsible for some word changes, though they will probably say they are only reflecting the language of the people. But it offends me that "Editorials" are now "Opinions." I like the responsibility of calling a page the Editorial page and letting the buck stop there. And renaming the section "Deaths," instead of the "Obituaries." Doesn't it imply a dumbing-down of language? We know what obituary means.

And low self-esteem—doesn't that ubiquitous term make your fillings ache? Bring back inferiority complex I say.

Yes, I know I'm on a tirade but we are all entitled to vent our spleen occasionally, and my venting is overdue.

The medical field is bad about these name changes too. I want to call *angina,* "an-gí-na" instead of "án-gin'a" as our doctors now do. I want to call "toxemia" by that venerable name, instead of "preeclampsia"—which nobody has ever heard of.

I don't want to get my daughter with a newborn baby a "doula"—that's the current word for what we used to call a "baby nurse." "Doula" has a faintly unsavory sound, for some reason. I was discussing this with a friend of mine, also a grandmother, who hit the nail right on the head.

"'Doula,'" she scoffed. "Back in my day, we just called it 'Help.'"

Journal Entry: Seagulls at Spring Break

The signs on the condo warn against feeding them. Now considered scavenger birds, seagulls are unwelcome at the places that feed and shelter those human winter birds from the North. In town, you see the seagulls hanging out at shopping centers, cruising across the paved parking lot in small cliques like teenage boys waiting for some action. The gulls, like those human counterparts, are ill at ease, wandering souls milling about, at a loss as to what to do next. They scan the pavement for a bit of French fry, or hamburger, or even a cannibal morsel of Chicken McNugget.

Seagulls look and act less like teenagers and are more themselves in their natural habitat on the beach, strolling the sand or diving the shallow waters for supper. The pounding surf seems to catapult these sea birds back to their Paleolithic roots. They recapture their lost dignity in this setting.

Something about this time of day—dusk, this time of year—March, this place—the beach and the gulls, combine into a special Spring Break. The evening sky tonight is streaked with pink and periwinkle at low tide. The ocean has belched up froth with the breaking waves tonight, like bubbles from a giant tub.

A large gathering of seagulls stand, shoulders toward the breaking surf, all facing the wind, motionless. Some are the wondrous laughing gulls with stylish black masks, mingling with their more pedestrian pearl and white kin, the herring gulls. The gulls don't even move as I wade into their midst. Maybe it's the grey sweat pants and jacket that camouflages and disguises me as one of them, except that I loom so large that I must look like a gull on steroids. But they do not seem to view me as an alien.

They stand in a lacy pattern of their own footprints in the sand. The individual triangular footprint is shaped like a tiny stingray or a kite. Hundreds of the prints in the powdery sand make a pattern akin to lace. My own solid footprint breaks the lace pattern.

We are the only creatures on the beach tonight as the light slips away. Their unblinking eyes stare off serenely toward the sun, sinking behind the beach houses. I love these birds.

I move through the seagulls as they stand sentinel to the south—waiting for what? I wonder. Where do they go when night comes and we retreat into beach houses and condos? You see the birds resting, floating on the surface of the ocean. Do they sleep floating on a rolling wave all night? The idea of perching in trees seems comic and ridiculous, most unseemly for the sea creatures.

I love the sound of the word. Gulls. That's what my Alabama cousins still call my sister and me, though we are long past youth. "How long will you gulls be able to stay in town?" they say when we return to Sumter County. Their accents are like some ancient, fragrant honey from my childhood.

My own daughter, raised in Mt. Pleasant near Charleston, and not accustomed to hearing her cousins' Alabama accents, called the birds *segals* when she was a child. The interesting pronunciation made me visualize them hobnobbing on the beach with Bernsteins and Cohens.

If you get the chance, walk on the beach before the summer crowds arrive and stand among these creatures. You will feel wonderfully collected when you watch the gulls circle, swoop, and spiral down with that remarkable rusty wheeling sound, light on the sand near you, and settle with silent, unblinking eyes toward the setting sun.

Rodin Has Left the Building

We had a treat in store when we went to see the Rodin exhibit this summer at the N.C. Museum of Art in Raleigh. The work of the artist some call the greatest sculptor since Michelangelo is stunning. The expressive bronze figures are monumental, and the fragment sculptures of hands are moving. I especially liked the unfinished marble pieces which seemed to be trying to free themselves from the stone, much like the unfinished statues of *Captives* by Michelangelo. Even *The Thinker,* his most familiar work, remains a powerful statement.

A nut for biographical information, I became fascinated with the artist's love affair, at age forty-three, with his nineteen-year-old apprentice, Camille Claudel. It was a passionate romance which lasted fifteen years. Camille advanced from student to collaborator to lover of the sculptor, who was at the height of his creative powers.

She modeled the hands and feet of some of his work and progressed to master sculptor in her own right. Camille inspired Rodin's erotic *The Kiss* and the less well-known *Eternal Springtime,* both extraordinarily passionate works even in today's market of hot images. Poor Camille went mad after their break-up and was institutionalized for the last thirty years of her life. A film, *Camille Claudel,* chronicles her descent into madness and fosters the idea that Rodin did indeed feed off of her imaginative soul to her eventual destruction.

Auguste Rodin enjoyed great success in his own lifetime. His fame and fortune were acquired not in some small degree by his savvy in merchandising his own work. Despite the scandal his most revolutionary works created, all were eventually accepted and revered. At the height of his popularity, he had some fifty-odd assistants to help him churn out his bronzes and marbles, which could be mail-ordered and created to suit the client's wishes, in large, medium, and small replicas.

The most unnerving part of the museum visit occurs, though, when you step into the gift shop adjacent to the exhibit. Prepare for the shameless world of merchandising.

Elvis, long one of the top modern merchandising images and product sponsors, may have a Frenchman, dead these eight decades, breathing down his neck.

In that shopping mode now? Good. Here are only a few of the available items.

For the homebody: A *Thinker* screen saver, apron, Christmas ornament, fridge magnet, coffee mug, magnetic clock, glassware, and my personal favorite: The Fliptomania book. The flipbook pages begin at the head of *The Thinker* and move down the body as you flip the pages. The last page ends at the stone feet of the statue, a roll of pink toilet paper nestled by his feet with the caption, "For *The Thinker* in all of us."

For the athlete: *Thinker* sports bottle, golf ball, Frisbee, yo-yo.

For the musician: A Rodin kazoo.

For the fashion-conscious: Rodin hat, lapel pin, golf shirt, key chain, necklace of copper, nickel, and brass geometric shapes which say "Think," and temporary tattoos.

For the workaholic: A *Thinker* address book, message cube, bookbag, pushpins, blank journal, vinyl folders, and a ballpoint pen featuring a floating miniature *Thinker* sculpture, drifting in front of the backdrop of the museum.

Overwhelmed, I narrowed to a choice between a bottle of spring water from Ontario with an image of *The Thinker* saying "I think I'm thirsty" for $1.25 and the funeral fan in the actual shape of *The Thinker*—on a stick for $2.00. A tough decision. I finally opted for the bottle of spring water. I think what I really needed was a cold compress.

The Christmas Spirits

Sponsored by the Civil War Roundtable, the Christmas Open House at the Bellamy Mansion featured more than authentic music and costumes. We could hear the music floating from the parlor as we started up the stairs to the porch of the antebellum house. It was a warm night; the front door was open. The Bellamy Mansion was decked in seasonal finery appropriate to December 1865, Della Robbia wreaths and bowers of magnolia leaves.

Inside we headed toward the music. "Southern Horizons" were said to be among the best musicians in the world of Civil War reenactment. The fiddler, crocheted gloves tucked neatly in the black sash of her hoop skirt, leaned into her instrument and struck up a lively polka. The man next to her played a guitar and in long black coat, string tie, and grey beard, looked to be a preacher. The third, a banjo player, wore the uniform of a Union soldier.

A young couple in period dress began to waltz to *Flow Gently Sweet Afton* and, as they swept toward us into the front parlor and past the Christmas tree, I couldn't help but notice that the woman seemed to radiate a certain light, a glow, despite the fact that her face was quite pale and haloed by dark hair parted in the middle, pulled back into the fashion of the time with a lace pouf on the chignon. The dress was extraordinary: lustrous silk in a rich wine color with yards and yards of swirling skirt. At her neck, a lace collar held by a cameo brooch. Garnet drop earrings swung as she turned.

Her tall partner was equally striking in the blue dress Union uniform with epaulets, brass buttons, and buckle. There was something about them. The two were so intent on each other that they danced as if there were no one else there.

After more polkas and reels, the couple stood in the corner sipping punch and leaning toward each other, whispering and smiling. We went over to tell them how much we enjoyed their dancing.

"We weren't supposed to be here," said the woman who introduced herself as Janine and her partner as Paul.

We looked puzzled.

"We were just touring the Bellamy Mansion this morning when someone said there was going to be an open house tonight with Civil War reenactors," she explained, brushing her dark hair back. "We laughed and said *we* were reenactors, had just been married in full 1865 period costumes, and were honeymooning here in Wilmington. The Bellamy House guide asked if we would come to the open house tonight and dance. So, here we are."

The handsome period outfits they wore were their wedding clothes. The looks they exchanged were pure honeymoon.

They had met briefly when they were teenagers. She was a Confederate reenactor at the Mary Seurat house when he first saw her through the window and later at the door. He was struck by the lovely girl with her dark hair and luminous eyes, who he said reminded him of a young Mary Seurat. But she was a Confederate reeanactor and he was a Union soldier. The reenactors at the Mary Seurat house did not take kindly to Yankees.

Twelve years later, they started dating. Within the year, they were married.

The music struck up a spirited polka and the newlyweds danced off into its rollicking turns. We were astounded . . . at the magical coincidence of it all, the luminous faces of the newlyweds, the exquisite costumes, the rightness of the Confederate and the Yankee clinging to each other in perfect harmony to the music.

"This old mansion must be very happy tonight," my friend said to me. I nodded.

And in my ear, the bride's last words to us as the couple danced away, "It all seems like a dream. Like a dream."

A Christmas Memoir in Three Parts

Part III: The Millennium Christmas

Christmas this year is both different—and the same. Some are not here to spend the joy of Christmas with us anymore, and we miss them sorely. But new family members, a daughter-in-law and a son-in-law, join the festivities now, and the littlest one, our granddaughter, is learning the family Christmas customs. Caroline is two and a half this holiday and is well on her way to seasonal indoctrination.

Her first Christmas' most memorable moment was when my sister came by to see the infant and we recorded the moment on camcorder. As she held the six-month-old Caroline beneath the twinkling Christmas tree and the camcorder whirred, the adorable baby looked up and—projectile vomited all over her great-aunt. It was indeed a Christmas memory caught on tape. The quintessential baby straight from *The Exorcist*, she really knows how to steal a scene. But it was the look on my sister's face that was the real Oscar winner.

Last Christmas in the drizzling rain, we bundled Caroline up to see the Santa at the Wrightsville Beach Fire Station. We were late and the good gentleman had stripped off the Santa coat and fake beard and was removing his Santa britches. He good-naturedly redressed, donned his beard, and rooted in his bag for a mesh Christmas stocking for the toddler. Caroline was smitten. Not with Santa, but with the dazzling red fire truck.

Our grandparents' gift last year to the toddler was something called a Mighty Marvel Mustang. It is a throwback toy from the fifties, a molded plastic beige horse which required no batteries or computer chips. It stands about three feet tall and is activated when the child bounces on the saddle seat and the legs splay outward, then contract—like a giant inchworm, moving forward in a jerking fashion.

I should have known better. Caroline is a slight child. The minimum weight necessary for the Mighty Marvel Mustang to move at all must be thirty-five pounds. Caroline did not make the cut. We put her astride the wonder horse. It was as still as a statue.

The stallion has been relegated to storage, along with the size-three clothes, the original Beatrix Potter books, and a copy of *The Secret Garden* she also received that Christmas. All overly ambitious gifts, even for a precocious grandchild.

This year the grandbaby has already seen Santa at an event in Cary called a "Breakfast with Santa." She did not hang back or whimper at the sight of the old elf, as some of the other children did, but strode confidently up to "The Man." He was a weather-beaten Santa but he sported a real beard (Caroline checked). Santa and Caroline had the same number of teeth—four. She crawled into his lap and whispered in his ear that this year she wanted a "twi-cycle."

Caroline has already helped with the Christmas decorations this year—in particular, the crèche, unwrapping the figures and asking me who each one is. She knows that those bearing gifts are Wise Men, though sometimes she calls them "wise guys." She recognizes that shepherds are the ones with the sheep. She knows that the Baby Jesus is the infant in the manger and that Christmas is *His* birthday.

She does not ask why there are *two* Marys. But one day, she will . . . and I hope I am there to explain.

May *your* Christmas be full of the joys of years past . . . and the dreams of those to come.

Photo by Jane Grant

N AN GRAHAM, born in Tallahassee, Florida, grew up in South Carolina, Alabama, and Georgia. She graduated from The University of North Carolina at Chapel Hill and received her graduate degree from The Citadel in Charleston. Except for a foray into Manhattan as a young adult, she has always lived in the South.

An instructor in English at UNC-Wilmington, Nan has been a biweekly commentator for the local public broadcasting station WHQR for the past six years. The familiar sign-off line to these commentaries is "Commentator Nan Graham is a lifelong Southerner." She is coauthor of a novel (set in the Depression in the North Carolina mountains) and hopes that the revision she is currently working on will be the final one.

Nan lives in Wilmington, North Carolina, with her husband, a West Highland terrier, and a semiferal cat named Sumter.